WRITE, WROTE, WRITTEN

Second Edition

Maureen S. Bogdanowicz

Mount Royal College
Calgary, Alberta

Formerly,
The University of Western Ontario
London, Ontario

Kendall/Hunt
Publishing Company
Dubuque, Iowa

Acknowledgments:

For permission to reprint copyright material grateful acknowledgment is made to H. M. H. Ltée and Anne Hébert for "The House on the Esplanade" from *Le Torrent*. This story first appeared in translation by Mona Scott Stoddard in *Queen's Quarterly*, 1953.

Printed in the United States of America

B   403611   01

Contents

Preface

Write, Wrote, Written has grown out of a concern about the place of student writing in a literature course. Students often need guidance in the process of writing essays and analyses. The content of a literature course is, and should be, literature. The literature classroom is not the place to spend an excessive amount of time teaching expository writing. It is the place where students learn to read literature critically. However, they are also expected to write critical essays and analyses. While learning "what to write" in the classroom, they must assimilate "how to write" elsewhere.

This book provides material students, particularly first year students, need to cope with their writing assignments. Examples are drawn from student work, both good and bad. In the Effective Writing Program at The University of Western Ontario and in the Learning Skills Centre at Mount Royal College, I have been teaching students how to get material down on paper in a suitable format. I have been teaching organization, presentation, and grammar to students who are unfamiliar with what writing essays and analyses is, and with why good form is necessary. The approach of this book is similar to the approach which has been used successfully with individual students.

This book is designed as a teaching tool. It provides the basics of good writing form and can be used in a classroom or tutorial to reinforce the basics. Exercises are provided for each skill and problem area. A student who is having problems with dangling modifiers, for example, can read the section on this problem and do the accompanying exercise. However, if more than a few students in a given class have this problem, the appropriate section of the book can be used as an in-class lesson.

My approach is logic- rather than rule-oriented. I feel it is enough for a student to *use* language correctly, even if he or she cannot recite the rules as they are applied. Thus, rules are presented, but logic is stressed.

I am grateful to the members of the English Department of the University of Western Ontario who have reviewed and commented on the book after using it in their classes. Their criticisms have been invaluable. In addition, I am grateful to the students who have allowed me to use their work. I would like to thank in particular S.E. McIntyre, E.S. Bradley, and M.E. François for allowing me to use their paragraphs in Chapter 2.

This revision of *Write, Wrote, Written* incorporates changes in the bibliographic conventions reflected in the 1984 *MLA Handbook for Writers of Research Papers*. Thus, substantive changes have been made to Part II: The Research Paper.

I would like to cite particular members of the University of Western Ontario English department for their advice and support: S.J. Adams, M.M. Brown, T.J. Collins, D.S. Hair, M.T. Neill, and C.E. Sanborn. Special thanks must be paid to Sue Desmond without whose typographical skills this book would not have been presentable.

Maureen Bogdanowicz
Calgary, Alberta

PART I

The Essay

CHAPTER 1

The Expository Essay

There are three kinds of essay writers. The first know all the rules and can write structurally sound essays on demand. Often, however, these writers have nothing imaginative to say. The second are enthusiastic about the topic and have countless interesting things to say, but present arguments in such random fashion that the logic of what is said is lost. The third combine enthusiasm and imagination with a disciplined presentation and make interesting points well. The third are successful essay writers.

You have been assigned to write an essay. What should you say? How should you say it? Where do you begin? There *must* be a correct way to do this assignment. You are not the only one in this dilemma. You should not allow yourself to be defeated before you even begin. Writing an essay may not be your idea of a good time or the way you would like to spend the weekend. Nevertheless, you may find yourself devoting increasing amounts of your "leisure time" to writing essays. It is not play; it is work; it is a discipline. However, essay writing does not have to be torture. It can be exciting and rewarding if you channel your energies and produce an essay, not just *x* number of words.

WHAT IS AN ESSAY?

The function of the essay is implicit in the derivation of the word itself. The word "essay" is derived from the French verb *essayer,* "to try." An essay is an attempt. In the case of an expository essay, the attempt is to prove a point or a thesis. The type of essay under discussion here, then, is defined as a formal exposition of a thesis. Bear this definition of the expository essay in mind as you formulate your essay, and the procedures to be followed in getting your arguments down on paper will become second nature to you. Remember, you are not writing a short story or a poem; you are making critical arguments and supporting them.

WHAT TO SAY

Before you can propose, prove, and expand on anything at all, you have to know your material. You cannot write about something which is unfamiliar to you. If you plan to write an essay about a particular text, it is necessary to read, re-read, and think about the assigned text before you can even hope to formulate ideas about it. After reading and re-reading a work and formulating ideas about it, you must analyze your ideas, retaining some and discarding others. Analyze your material before you even think about writing your essay. You cannot even choose your essay topic until you have done this preliminary analysis. You may decide that an alternative topic interests you more than the first "blind" choice. If, however, you choose your topic first and then gear your preliminary reading of the work to a search for material on that topic, you will lose any sense of the whole. In effect, you see only what you are looking for and miss other valuable material. If, for example, you look only for evidence of "the colour green" in *Sir Gawain and the Green Knight,* you may well overlook the importance of "the quest." Think about the work as a whole and then, *and only then,* think of an aspect of the work—a topic.

Often you will be given a choice of essay topics. Some, of course, will appear to be more appealing at first sight than others. You must look beyond a topic *per se* and think of the application of it to the literary work, since whatever the topic, you must deal with it within the context of the literature. Avoid getting off on the wrong foot by *first* choosing a topic and *then* focusing your reading of the text on *only* that topic. Know the whole book, play, or poem before you write about it. There is more to *King Lear* than "madness" and more to Margaret Laurence's *The Diviners* than "the narrative technique."

A formula for a successful essay is the following:

1. Know the primary material.
2. Select a topic.
3. Re-read the literature with the topic in mind.
4. If necessary, consult secondary material.
5. Focus on the topic and develop a logical analysis of appropriate selections from the text.

If step 5 proves impossible, go back to step 2 and select a different topic.

HOW MUCH TO SAY

If you do the appropriate preparatory work, you could write volumes on your topic. Initially you may feel that you have too little to say, but, if you have truly considered your topic and your text, your problem should be having too much rather than too little to say. Review your material and your topic. How can you do them justice in the number of pages you are allowed?

Remember the definition of an essay. It is a formal exposition of a *thesis*. It proves a point. This definition leads to the crucial decision to be made before you write a word. What *point* are you proving? This point is your thesis. Your essay is an organized explication of this thesis. In your "essay" you "attempt" to prove your point. Think again about the definition of an essay. It is not random thoughts on a topic; it is a formal explication of a thesis.

Your topic is a broad subject; your thesis is narrow. Often the topic is assigned; a thesis is sometimes, but not often, assigned. For example, you are required to write a 1500 word essay on "Imagery in *Macbeth*." If you think you can write about all the imagery (bird, animal, blood, light/dark, plant, clothing, colour) in *Macbeth* in 1500 words, you will allow yourself a paragraph per image. Your essay will amount to a "skip through *Macbeth*," pointing out images along the way. Is this approach what you want? Of course not.

Consider the graphic representation of the formal essay on the next page. Note that an essay must have broad bases on which it is balanced at both the beginning and the end. In your *Macbeth* essay, for example, you have a broad topic, imagery; you must choose a narrow thesis.

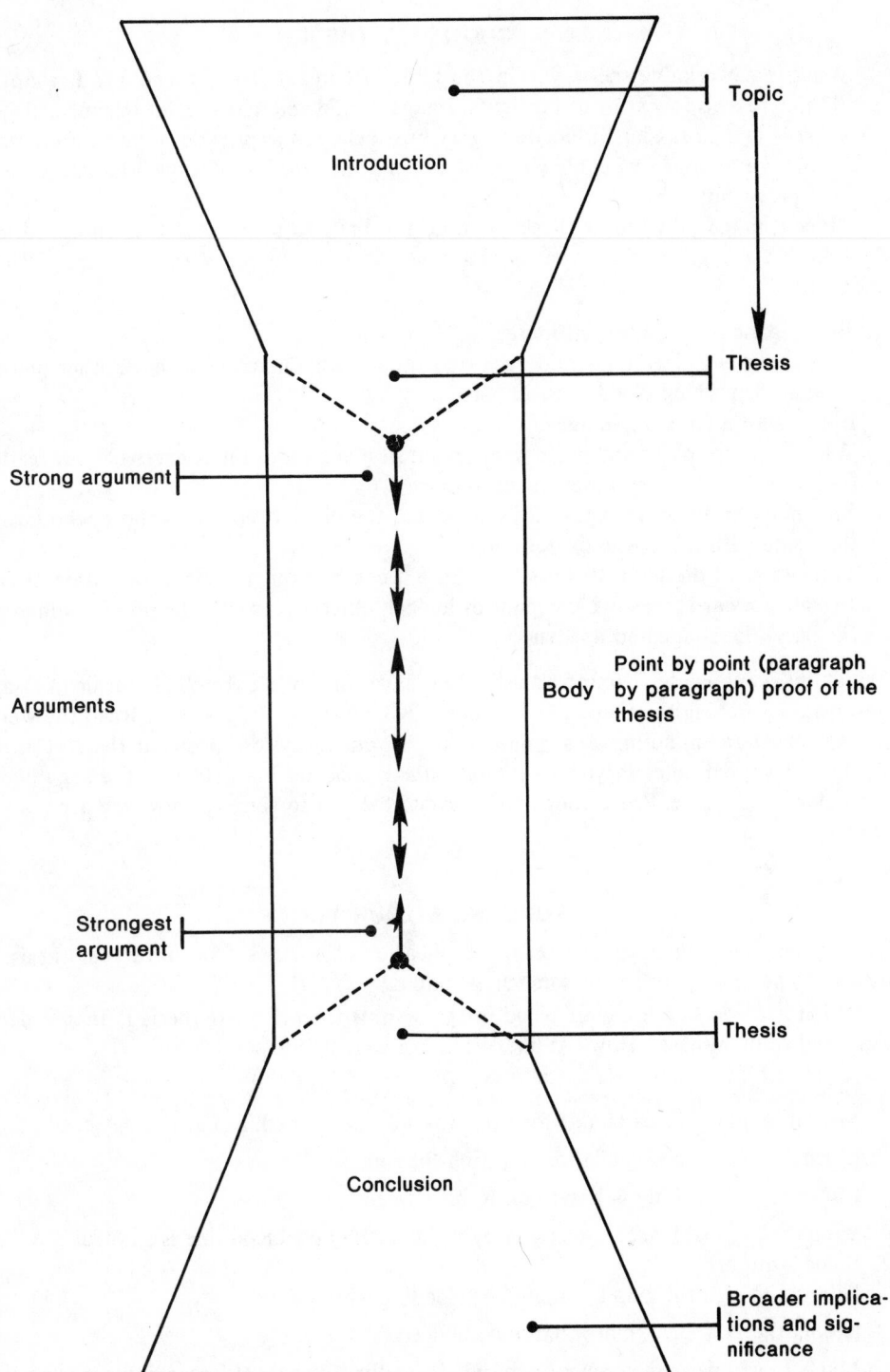

Introduction

Topic

Thesis

Strong argument

Arguments

Body

Point by point (paragraph by paragraph) proof of the thesis

Strongest argument

Thesis

Conclusion

Broader implications and significance

CHOOSE A THESIS

What is a workable thesis within the topic of "Imagery in *Macbeth*"? Perhaps the most logical thing to do is focus on one particular image. Could you manage, for instance, blood imagery in *Macbeth?* Is a discussion of blood imagery broad enough to provide sufficient material and still narrow enough to be manageable within your page and word limitations? Examine the imagery. It should prove suitable.

"Blood imagery" is not a thesis. You do not have to prove that there is blood imagery in *Macbeth*. That is given. So—what is your thesis? What do you want to prove? What are the possibilities?

1. Blood is the most important image.
   This thesis is still pretty broad because it involves comparison with all other images as well as analysis proving blood most important.
2. Blood is an interesting image.
   Whether or not blood and blood imagery interest you is not the concern of your reader. Forget the "I like" or "this reminds me of" habit.
3. The image of blood changes meaning within the play. It contrasts those who have right on their side with those who exercise might.
   This is a good thesis for this essay because it can be explicated in 1500 words. It is a strong, straight-forward thesis which requires logical, objective proof. The proof is inherent in both the play's language and its structure.

At this point you have found a thesis. You have gone over a very high hurdle in essay writing. However, just finding the thesis is not enough. Now you have to prove it. Read the work (in this case, the play) again, noting what you can use in your essay to prove your thesis. Can you prove it? Make marginal notes in your text. Be critical; consider both sides of the argument. Debate with a devil's advocate. Prove your thesis beyond a doubt to yourself; now you are ready to prove it to someone else.

ORGANIZE YOUR PROOF

Remember—your essay is a formal explication of a thesis. You have your thesis. Now explicate it. The task is not so awesome as it sounds.

What are you saying about blood imagery in *Macbeth?* Your thesis is that it depicts both might and right. Where? How? Who? What are your major points?

1. Blood—right
   Macbeth fights (sheds blood) for right (in defense of the king) at the outset of the play.
   Bloody wounds "become" those fighting for right.
   Life-blood of the king is passed on to his descendants.
   Banquo's sons will wear the crown by right—Banquo's blood line is rightful.
2. Blood—might
   Killing the rightful king by might is "bloody business."
   Killing the king is a "more than bloody deed."
   Macbeth will wear the crown by might (by spilling blood). His sons will not wear it by right.

The ends of the spectrum of blood imagery seem provable. Are there other implications in the blood imagery? If you can work these implications out in an outline, you have a workable plan for your essay.

TITLE

Before outlining your material you must find a title for your essay. The title should indicate what literary piece you are discussing as well as imply your thesis. A title like "Essay #1" is no help to your reader; nor is "English Essay." Something like "Shakespeare's *Macbeth*" is certainly more helpful, but you must be even more precise. A suitable title might be "Might, Right, and Blood in *Macbeth*." Your title, in this case, indicates the work and the line of discussion you have chosen. Since your title is the first thing a reader sees, why not make a good impression from the beginning?

OUTLINE THE ESSAY

The outline is a means of organizing the material for your essay in such a way that the flow and direction of your arguments can be charted. In effect, the outline is a skeleton of the essay; it provides form and structure. If the outline is sound, the essay will likewise be sound. Once you have organized your material in outline form, you have a plan for the essay itself. You always know where you are in your argument, as well as where you have been and where you are going. In the outline you decide *what* to say; thus, in writing the essay you need to concentrate on *how* to make your argument clear, not on *what* proof to use. The result should be an organized essay.

There are two formats for an outline: the sentence and the point formats. As their names imply, the former is less abbreviated than the latter. Generally, the point outline is preferable since it is less cumbersome and forces you to condense your ideas in a phrase. Remember, however, that too much abbreviation can lead to confusion. If your outline is too sparse it may exclude necessary material. The outline is for *your* use. Find a balance that is suitable for you.

Remember the diagram of the essay structure. The body of the essay is a point by point proof of the thesis. Your outline lists your points (and subpoints) in the order in which you choose to deal with them. When you write your essay, you expand your points into paragraphs. Look at the following sample outline for the *Macbeth* essay:

TITLE—Might, Right, and Blood in *Macbeth*
Introduction
Thesis: The image of blood changes meaning in the play. It contrasts those who have right on their side with those who exercise might.

I. It is praiseworthy to shed blood for a rightful cause.
    A. "Wounds become" a defender of the rightful king. (might for right)
        1. Act I, scene ii is a discussion of honour.
        2. Macbeth is promoted, honoured for defending king.

II. It is possible to exercise power or might against rightful authority.
   A. Killing the king.
      1. "Bloody business" (II.1.48).
      2. "More than bloody deed." (II.IV.21).
   B. Fulfillment of prophecy: "Macbeth shall be king."
      1. He is king by misusing might and shedding blood.
III. Shedding blood upsets the rightful blood line for the monarchy.
   A. Donalbain's "fountain of blood/Is stopped, its very source is stopped." (II.iii.93–4).
   B. Donalbain becomes Macbeth's "bloody cousin" (III.i.29).
      1. relation of the king.
      2. in line to be murdered: "The nearer in blood/The nearer "bloody" (II.iii.136–7).
   C. Macbeth's blood line will not produce a king by either might or right.
      1. Witches' prophecy.
      2. Macbeth's dream of Banquo (IV.i.123–124).
   D. Additional blood (Banquo's) does not make might right.
IV. The result of shedding blood wrongly is "bloody" guilt and more bloodshed.
   A. Smear Duncan's grooms with blood—false guilt.
   B. Blood on the face of Banquo's murderer—guilt.
   C. "Bloody" hand of night cannot hide guilt (III.ii.48).
   D. Lady Macbeth's sleepwalking.
      1. Wash blood (guilt) from hand (II.ii.59–60).
   E. "Kill the king"—bloody instructions. Kill Banquo (Banquo in "bloody distance" to Macbeth) (III.i.116).
      1. guilt—Banquo heard prophecy; he suspects Macbeth's guilt.
      2. Banquo is in line to be killed.
      3. lineage—Banquo's sons will be kings. Battle results—more bloodshed.
 V. The bloody cycles continue and blood-right prevails.
   A. Macbeth's sons never wear the crown.
   B. "Blood will have blood." (III.iv.122).
      1. Might will have guilt.
      2. Right will have might.
      3. Guilt will have might.
   C. Duncan, the rightful king, ultimately has might and right.
      1. "Who would have thought the old man to have had so much *blood* in him?" (V.i.35–37).
         a. After right is killed by might, guilt lives.
         b. Right prevails. Duncan has *right* even when dead.
   D. The initial paradox of "fair is foul and foul is fair" is ultimately expanded to "right is might and might is right."

Conclusion
Thesis restated: Blood imagery is a touchstone for the merits of the actions in *Macbeth*. In their proceedings, characters are exercising either might (wrongly) or right (rightly).

MOVE FROM THE OUTLINE TO THE ESSAY

The worst is over. You have a thesis; you know it is provable; you know how you are going to prove it. You can write your essay.

It is usually a good idea to "sleep on" your outline before attacking the essay itself. You want to be logical and objective when you write. Allow time to work on your essay in phases: organization, writing, revision. If your essay is due on Friday, you should organize your material in outline form by the preceding Monday at the latest. You are probably too close to your material at the moment when you finish working on your outline. There is a lot going on in your head; the outline and your material are very immediate. If you distance yourself in time from your work and *then* go over your outline, you stand a better chance of detecting any flaws in your logic.

After a break, go back to your outline. Revise it if necessary. You are in an enviable position. You know what you are going to argue, how you are going to prove your thesis, and in what order your arguments will come so you do not need to juggle facts and sound insecure as you write. You will not find yourself writing "as I shall prove later," "as I stated earlier," "as I hope to prove." Rather than promising your reader what will come and reminding him or her of what you have already proven, you can be assertive and proceed with your proof.

As you write page one, you know what is coming on pages three, five, seven, and so on. You can save arguments for where they are most needed and thus avoid rambling. In addition, you can disengage yourself as a first person participant in the essay ("I think," "I hope," "It seems to me"), and get on with an objective analysis of the literature. Since you know your thesis is manageable and your proof logical, you can be assertive and avoid the subjunctive mood and the passive voice ("It might be proven that . . .").

THE INTRODUCTION

The importance of your introduction cannot be overemphasized. It is here that you interest your reader and provide a motivating force for the essay. You have a great deal of leeway in your introduction. You set the rules and standards against which the rest of your essay should be judged. Here you set your task, a task which your outline has shown you can fulfill. *You* are setting the limits of your essay. Do it well and your essay should be successful.

Your introduction starts broadly with the topic and narrows to the thesis. In a short essay this movement may not always be necessary; you might start with your thesis, especially if the thesis has been assigned. The introduction is not lengthy; 50 to 75 words is usually satisfactory.

Do you remember the mental gymnastics you went through to arrive at your thesis? *You* went through them; your reader did not. Because your reader may not have followed the same train of thought you employed, you must indicate how you have decided that, out of all the possibilities, *blood* is the most suitable image for discussion. Now you can state your thesis. Do not make apologies about or waste words on space and time permitting or not permitting; be aggressive and optimistic. You *know* you can prove your thesis. Give that impression from the outset. Narrow your topic to a thesis; state your thesis; then prove it in the body of your essay.

The introduction to the *Macbeth* essay might well follow this diagram:

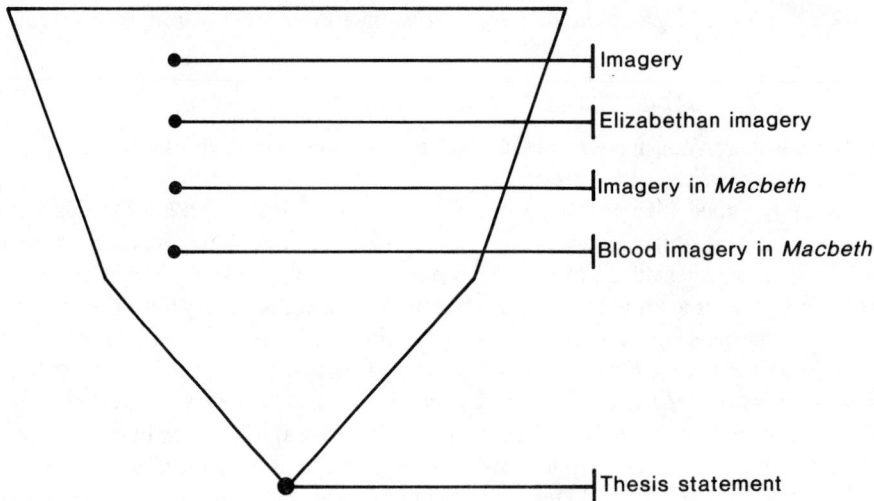

Notice that the work in question is introduced *by name* in the introduction. You are moving from the work in general to a specific aspect of it and thus providing an environment for the thesis statement.

THE BODY OF THE ESSAY

The body of the essay is a point by point explication of the thesis. There are several ways of arranging these points. Logic is imperative. At the same time, you should start and end your essay with strong arguments, and move smoothly through your presentation.

Some acceptable types of arrangement are the following:

1. Chronological development;
2. Cause and effect development;
3. Proof by reasons;
4. Proof by example;
5. Refutation of common interpretations or of critics' views;
6. Development by characteristics of a work;
7. Thesis, antithesis, synthesis.

(The discussion of types of paragraph development in the following chapter discusses modes of exposition. Refer to Chapter 2 if necessary.) Different arrangements are suitable in different situations. Sometimes a combination of arrangements may be employed.

One type of arrangement which is *not* suitable in an essay is the "book report." Remember that you are not the only person who has read the work. Certainly your reader knows, for example, the plot of *Macbeth*. Do not insult his or her intelligence by reciting the plot. Do not waste your and your reader's time and energy. You must make every word count as proof of your thesis; plot summaries do not count. Focus on what you are trying to prove and prove it.

THE CONCLUSION

Graphically, the conclusion is a mirror image, but not a repetition, of the introduction. To conclude an essay you should start with a narrow point (the thesis) and then broaden to wider implications of the thesis or the topic. In other words, the conclusion broadens out to further considerations. Your conclusion should be as short as possible. Generally three or four sentences comprise a concluding paragraph. *Avoid* perfunctory, one-sentence tags as conclusions. Your thesis has been proven in the body of the essay; do not attempt to re-prove it in the conclusion. Rather, rephrase and expand the thesis.

Many unsuccessful conclusions begin with "Therefore we can see . . .," or "In conclusion it might be said . . .," or "I hope you agree with me that. . . ." Be confident about your work. If *you* do not believe that you have proven your thesis and only "hope that it is clear that . . .," *who* will believe you?

Your conclusion might well conform to the following illustration:

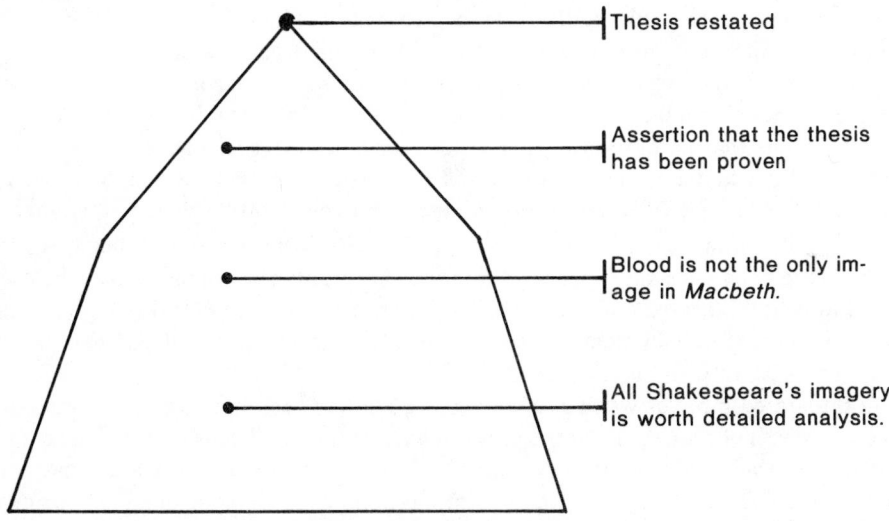

Your essay now has a broad base on which to rest. If you have completed each phase of organizing your material well, your essay should be structurally sound.

PROOFREAD

Before you submit a final draft, proofread carefully. The best way is to proofread aloud or have someone else proofread for you. The final responsibility, however, rests with you. Make neat corrections and submit your essay *on time*.

CHAPTER 2

Paragraphs

Organization is the backbone of good writing. You know you must outline the points of any argument, especially the arguments in an essay. When you move from the outline to formal prose, your points must be differentiated. Thus, your writing must be organized in paragraphs. This organizing is done out of consideration for the reader. Even the most intelligent and literate of readers cannot hold pages and pages of print in his or her mind if the material is in one block. In writing analyses or essays, you are presenting quite a lot of material. In order for your argument to be clear, the material must be divided into manageable blocks which, put together, comprise your work.

A paragraph is not normally as short as a single sentence, nor is it usually as long as 500 words. It is a group of sentences which explores one, *and only one* idea. In other words, it develops one thought. The point which is being developed is indicated in the topic sentence. The paragraph goes on to expand, clarify, explain, illustrate, or prove the assertion of the topic sentence. Thus, a paragraph is comprised of several sentences making up an organic whole.

Do not be deceived by your handwritten draft. The fact that your *writing* covers several lines does not mean that the topic has been developed and the paragraph is complete. It is often surprising to writers that paragraphs which seemed long on the written page are much shorter on the typed page. Your material, not the amount of space you have used, dictates when a paragraph is finished. When you have fully developed one idea, end your paragraph and start another.

Generally the initial sentence introduces the "topic" of the paragraph, but this rule is not iron-clad. The topic sentence may appear later in the paragraph, sometimes even as the concluding sentence. However, it must exist. A paragraph must have a topic, or central thought, because the paragraph must be the development of a single thought. If it is not, the alleged paragraph is only a group of sentences thrown together at random.

In an integrated piece of writing, a connecting link between paragraphs is mandatory. The link picks up a chain of thought from the preceding paragraph and continues it. The continuation may consist of further analyses along the same lines, or it may move toward new material and a new outlook. At all times, a change from or continuation of the chain of thought is evident in the links between paragraphs. A missing link is as much a problem to a reader as it was to Darwin. There is, then, a link between the conclusion of one paragraph and the beginning of the next.

As a good writer, you should develop a repertoire of pivotal or "gesture" words, phrases, or links. For instance, you may sometimes find it necessary to repeat a key word from the preceding paragraph. At other times, conjunctive adverbs may serve as transitional signposts. Guide your reader from one idea to the next.

Remember that your reader may not make the same mental jumps that you do. A link that is apparent to you may not be striking to a reader. Consider the uses of the following transitions. Which are synonymous? Are there subtle differences of meaning? If so, what are they?

because of	therefore	although
due to	consequently	even though
	thus	even if
furthermore	indeed	in spite of
moreover	in fact	despite

When would you use these links and others like them? Remember—it is not enough merely to provide a link between thoughts, concepts, and discussions; you must provide the appropriate link, and use it correctly.

Note the movement of the following sample paragraph:

Topic:

authority,
implication of lack
of freedom for
individuals

explanation
discussion

focus on most
important point;
preparation for
movement into next
paragraph.

The seventeenth century in England witnessed a struggle between king and parliament, a struggle between the ideas of absolutism and of a limited monarchy, a revolt, in other words, against supreme authority resting in one man. Within this general struggle in the realm of ideas, everything from absolute monarchy to anarchy was advocated. One of the outstanding features of the period (especially the years between 1640 and 1660) was the numerous pamphlets and more scholarly works which were written in support of one side or another. Hobbes and Locke held the first place among these writers, but this is not to forget the others: Winstanley, Lilburne, Milton, and Harrington, to mention only a few. Among the topics of frequent discussion were the contract theory, interpreted to justify both absolutism and sovereignty as ultimately residing in the people; classical republicanism; and democracy with almost a communist twist.

Perhaps the most frequently debated single issue concerned the rights of individuals. . . .

Topic:

Here the topic is evident in the topic sentence. A lucid and logical discussion follows in which the implications of the topic are explored. A concluding comment focuses on the most important point and paves the way for the introduction of the next paragraph which will go on to explore a new, but related, topic.

MODES OF EXPLICATION

There are various patterns by which the discussion, argument, evidence, clarification, or analysis implicit in your paragraph can be arranged. These are modes or types of explication. While the formula inherent in each example is not rigid, a consideration of the different types of explication does provide a starting point in an analysis of paragraph writing.

No one mode is used consistently. A piece of writing is made up of many paragraphs and their formulae vary. Your *purpose* in writing any given paragraph and the material with which you are dealing should dictate the mode of explication which is most suitable.

Seven types of explication will be discussed here: explication from general to specific; by example; by definition or equation; by categorization; by classification; by comparison; and by refutation or modification. You may use any or all of these in a series of paragraphs. In fact, you may merge types of explication in a single paragraph. Bear in mind your purpose and your material and express your information in the most suitable format.

1. Explication from General to Specific

The title of this method of explication implies its movement. When you employ this formula you initiate the paragraph with a general statement or present a general situation, followed by a discussion or presentation of specific details or situations which are smaller parts of the general statement. Generally, an introductory paragraph of an essay follows this pattern: from the topic (general) to the thesis (specific). On the one hand, you may end with a new or refined generalization about your material, thus bringing the discussion full circle. On the other hand, you may end with a particular point, providing a bridge into the next paragraph. Your next paragraph may employ another form of explication in a discussion of the particular point you are expanding.

William Makepeace Thackeray's *Vanity Fair* presents a vivid depiction of English society of the early nineteenth century, and of such particularized places as Brussels on the eve of Waterloo. Thackeray takes as his sphere of interest the upper classes and deliberately narrows his subject to the behavior of individuals within the family circle. He deals with life in the drawing room, and takes it upon himself to explore the shallowness, cruelty, greed, and hypocrisy of the socially privileged. Thackeray points out that "we do not claim to rank among the military novelists. Our place is with the non-combatants." Thus, in this "novel without a hero" one views the society of England against the backdrop of the Napoleonic Wars, paying little attention to the actual battles. While history goes on, life goes on as well.

This writer has moved from a general historical era, nineteenth century England during the Napoleonic Wars, to upper class society. The movement is then from society in general to the drawing room—from general to specific.

2. Explication by Examples

Using this method, you clarify the topic sentence by citing examples which illustrate or substantiate the topic. In an extended and integrated piece of writing, these examples may be expanded individually in further paragraphs.

Margaret Laurence's Manawaka is not only a place but also a representation of the author's point of reference. Manawaka, in both a physical and psychological sense, is a world from which each of the five Laurence women under discussion tries successfully or unsuccessfully to escape. Hagar Shipley, a product of the pioneering community, remains for some time, but leaves when she is middle-aged. Rachel Cameron leaves to go to college in the city, but is forced to return upon the death of her father, eventually getting away permanently at the age of thirty-five. Her sister, Stacey, leaves at nineteen. Both Vanessa MacLeod and Morag Gunn escape to the city to attend university in Winnipeg.

In this paragraph, an assertion is made in the topic sentence. Examples follow to provide proof of the initial assertion. The writer has cited examples of the actions of Laurence's individual heroines to prove the general contention that they all attempt to escape, physically and psychologically, from Manawaka. The essay may go on to assess each woman's level of success.

3. Explication by Definition or Equation

This type of explication is the means by which an unusual term or phenomenon is made clear. Often in literary essays, this pattern is used to explicate a symbol or image. The clarification may involve straight definition. Sometimes, however, this definition may take the form of equating the unclear term with something concrete, followed by analysis of the definition or equation.

> The reader of Camus' *The Plague* explores with the author the course of a mass pestilence and its effects on the society involved. Through the image of a plague, Camus has produced a concrete concept of evil. The good that prevailed in a society prior to the advent of a plague is pitted against this evil. In the eyes of Camus, the gradual descent of evil upon a basically good society, its prolonged affinity to that society, and finally its gradual expulsion, do, in fact, leave an imprint. The evil is of a parasitic nature, drawing sustenance from that to which it has attached itself.

Here the writer has defined an evil as a mass pestilence. In equating evil with the concrete image of a plague, the writer has intensified the definition. He or she may go on to analyze individual aspects of and incidents relating to the plague and the evil associated with it.

Please note that you should avoid trite dictionary definitions in your essay. If you find it necessary to define a term, note the applicability of the definition to your discussion. The definition should be useful for a term in the context in which you are using it. In addition, you cannot define one term by using a variation of the same term. This "definition" is a tautology. In saying, for example, that irony is ironic, you give no helpful information. Only functional definitions are warranted in your explications.

4. Explication by Categorization

By means of this method you delegate material to a category and then illustrate its suitability for that category. You might categorize, for example, persons, places, things, events or images. In some cases, mere categorization is not sufficient; the category itself must be explained or defined.

> Among Shakespeare's major female roles, those of Juliet, Desdemona, and Cordelia are what might be termed "Helpless Victims of Love." It might be argued that Desdemona and Cordelia show initiative and firmness in their original "stands," and that they determine their own fates considerably. Juliet too must take the first steps in her clandestine arrangements with Romeo. In the end, however, each heroine is led not by rational choice, even for self-preservation, but by the fatal necessity to serve the man she loved.

This writer has labelled the category, delegated persons to it, and gone on to indicate the aptness of the categorization. Three "Helpless Victims of Love" are identified and some rationale for their placement in the category is given. The following paragraphs might deal with each character individually, and, consequently, unify the presentation. The essay may then go on to explore other categories.

5. Explication by Classification or Division

This mode is similar to the "general to specific" mode in that a general category initiates the paragraph and particular instances are elicited from the general category. However, in this case the data are more exact. A general category is cited and then divided into parts. Rather than moving from the general to one specific point, the writer deals with two or more specific instances or examples.

> There are three kinds of essay writers. The first knows all the rules and can write structurally sound essays on demand. Often, however, these writers have nothing imaginative to say. The second are enthusiastic about the topic and have countless interesting things to say, but present arguments in such random fashion that the logic of what is said is lost. The third combine enthusiasm and imagination in a disciplined presentation and make interesting points well. The third are successful essay writers.

This writer has broken down the general category of essay writer and has divided it into three parts, each an offshoot of the general category. The individual parts comprise the whole and the classifications are exact.

6. Explication by Comparison

In this instance the writer cites the similarities and differences between or among things. Similarities must be discussed before the writer focuses on contrasting elements. By this means, a basis for comparison is established before divergences are noted. There are two ways of developing this type of analysis. The first may be used in preparing material, while the second is preferable in the actual essay.

The former approach describes one side of the coin fully and then focuses entirely on the other side. The same order of points is followed for both sides. The following is an abbreviated illustration:

Item A introduced; Item B introduced

X applied to item A
Y applied to item A
Z applied to item A

Item A summarized

Item B re-introduced

X applied to item B
Y applied to item B
Z applied to item B

Item B summarized; Item A mentioned

The presentation is logical, but demands, for example, that a reader retain "X applied to item A" until he or she gets to "X applied to item B." Your reader, rather than you, the writer, makes the necessary connections. After arranging your material according to this formula, rewrite it in a second approach to comparison.

The second approach to explication by comparison considers each point applied to both sides of the coin. In this case, the result should be a balanced antithetical presentation. Consider the following abbreviated illustration:

Item A introduced; Item B introduced

X applied to item A
X applied to item B
statement of similarities and/or differences

Y applied to item A
Y applied to item B
statement of similarities and/or differences

Z applied to item A
Z applied to item B
statement of similarities and/or differences

Conclusion: comparison of item A and item B

Here the writer provides links in the comparison. Less is demanded of the reader structurally.

Balance is crucial; weigh each item in your comparison. Establish similarities and move on to differences, if they exist.

> Although *Hamlet* and *Macbeth* are both tragedies, the motives and achievements of their respective heroes contrast in several respects. In the opening scenes of both plays the heroes are prevailed upon by supernatural forces. While, in response, Hamlet is moody and uncertain, Macbeth is bold and aggressive. Hamlet, a man of words, is an intellectual and a poet; Macbeth, on the other hand, is a leader, a man of action. As the plays progress, Hamlet is called to action by his father's ghost, but is paralyzed, whereas Macbeth is internally driven to action which, while decisive, is ultimately destructive. While Hamlet is motivated by a desire to re-establish order and justice in his kingdom. Macbeth is controlled by greed and ambition which breed chaos and disorder throughout the land.

In this paragraph, the writer has shown similarities and differences between two Shakespearean heroes. The comparison is carried out point by point; Hamlet and Macbeth are compared throughout the paragraph. Individual points of comparison may be developed in later paragraphs.

7. Explication by Refutation or Modification

In writing this type of explication you take the reader from a common supposition or frame of reference to an opposing view. You then go on to support the opposing view. It is necessary for you to acknowledge the point you are refuting and to refute the point rationally. Dismissing something out of hand as being "crazy" or "unwarranted" does not effectively refute a point.

> James Joyce, a product of Irish Catholic Dublin, has become one of the most influential of twentieth century literary artists. He, along with D.H. Lawrence, shows the profound effect of Sigmund Freud on twentieth century concepts of the inner workings

of the mind. As a result, it has sometimes been proposed that Joyce's work is unintelligible because of his concern almost exclusively with the inner workings of the mind. Each of James Joyce's works, however, follows an outline and is constructed around a definite framework. Consideration of the framework and structure will lead to acuity in an understanding of the work. Such is the case with his short story "Grace" in *Dubliners*.

Here the writer refutes the belief that Joyce's narrative technique is without structure. The essay will illustrate the refutation with reference to a particular work by Joyce.

In some instances the argument or refutation may come full circle, refuting a point, but then refining or modifying the initial point. In other words, this refutation modifies, rather than dismisses, a common belief.

As much as all of Shakespeare's female characters are interesting, and some indeed very forceful as well, it cannot be claimed that he draws a tragic heroine as definitively as he does a tragic hero. Neither Juliet nor Cleopatra, for instance, who might be designated as tragic heroines are alone paramount in the structures of *Romeo and Juliet* and *Anthony and Cleopatra*. The role of each is dependent on that of her male opposite, and neither stands out in the way that Hamlet, Lear, or Othello do in their individual dilemmas. However, in many cases, by their subtly supporting or catalytic dramatic functions, the Shakespearean female roles are more interesting than the male. They say much about the playwright and the times, about the considerable resourcefulness of the women of the Elizabethan era, and about the ways in which their influence was exercised.

This writer has refuted the claim that Shakespeare's dramatic heroines are as definitive as his heroes. However, the heroines are not dismissed. The terms "definitive" and "tragic heroine" have been modified. The female roles are redefined as influential and complex. The essay will go on to prove this allegation.

THE PARAGRAPH REVIEWED

The paragraph is an important element in writing and, as such, must relate material well. Thus, how you write something is as important as what you write. An expository technique exists for each of a variety of purposes for relating material. If the techniques are well chosen, the piece of writing fulfills its purpose.

Modes of explication must be integrated to avoid boring prose. You should not drive a car in one gear; you should not write a series of paragraphs in one mode. Consequently, you must consider the purpose of a piece of writing and the nature of your material and then employ the most satisfactory devices of explication.

Regardless of what types of explication you use, you must always write in *complete* paragraphs, each consisting of a topic sentence and a development of that topic. A series of short, abrupt, underdeveloped paragraphs gives an unpleasant staccato effect, whereas pages and pages of lengthy paragraph intimidate (not to mention confuse) even the best of readers.

If you have something worth writing, write it clearly. If you do not have something worth discussing, why write anything at all? You need both content and form. The content you get in class, in the library, and from your own native intelligence; the form is your own production.

EXERCISE 1

The following are two paragraphs from an expository essay. The first is presented intact; the second, however, is fragmented. The selection deals with interpretations of William Faulkner's *The Sound and the Fury*. Read the first paragraph and determine the direction of the argument. Reassemble the second in the most logical sentence order. Note that the reference in sentence #4 is to a work in the "Works Cited" listing at the end of the paper. The reference to Evelyn Scott's article is given below.

Paragraph 1

Because Faulkner's style in *The Sound and the Fury* is so obscure, the novel is left wide open for misinterpretation. The plot is related in the first section and then retold from three other points of view. Even in its repetition, however, Faulkner's presentation of content is not necessarily logical. As a result, some critics resort to graphic depictions, such as guides to scene shifts and charts of the chronological order of events in the novel, before they begin their analysis of the story. An example of this is Edmond L. Volpe's *A Reader's Guide to William Faulkner*.

Note that the reference in sentence #4 is to a work in the "Works Cited" at the end of the paper. The reference is given on the next page.

Paragraph 2

Sentence Number	Logical Placement
1. Benjy, Ms. Scott says, is a Christ figure, and, at the same time, is like Adam.	_____
2. Other critics do not consider the parts as they relate to the whole novel.	_____
3. While her claims about Benjy are acceptable, she nevertheless passes over Quentin as simply "the last wealth of the family" who cannot accept that position.	_____
4. Evelyn Scott, in a critique of the book published the same year as *The Sound and the Fury,* is caught in the mistake of interpreting Benjy as the main figure in the book.	_____
5. Through the last section of the book, we see the story of the Compson family as a unit in respect to Yoknapatawpha County, according to Ms. Scott.	_____
6. Jason, she says, is a devil caught in a world of "petty, sadistic lunacy."	_____

Read the paragraphs again, reading the second in the order in which you have arranged it. Is the writing clear? How are the paragraphs linked? In the second paragraph, what are the internal transitions and links which dictate the order you have given it? Would you change or strengthen any transitions? Note that the paragraph as it stands in the exercise makes no sense at all. Your rearrangement has given the material structure and form. Organized material is clear, whereas random ordering of thoughts conveys nothing but confusion.

(suggested arrangement: 3, 1, 4, 2, 6, 5)

WORKS CITED

Scott, Evelyn. "On William Faulkner's *The Sound and the Fury*." *Twentieth Century Interpretations of* The Sound and the Fury. Ed. Michael H. Cowan. Englewood Cliffs: Prentice, 1968. 26–7.

EXERCISE 2

Put the following paragraph in order as you did in the previous example. In this exercise, you do not have an introductory paragraph from which to determine the movement of the argument. Find a viable starting point, and work from there.

Sentence Number	Logical Placement
1. In addition there is the appalling attitude of the book stores that relegate books by Canadian authors to a special section, generally at the back of the store, quaintly labelled CANADIANA.	_____
2. In all fairness to our authors, we must note the difficulties they face once their books have been published.	_____
3. This implies a dreadful lack of confidence in our literature, as though Canadian books were only for special tastes, or as though they might suffer from too close proximity with American or British books.	_____
4. For example, there is a discrepancy in price between McClelland and Stewart Limited's New Canadian Library Series and Palmer.	_____
5. Canadian books in paperback are still more expensive than American ones.	_____

Well, how did you do? Read the paragraph as it stood and then read it as you have arranged it. Is the difference striking? Would you, as a reader, prefer the structured or the unorganized presentation?

(suggested arrangement: 4, 1, 5, 3, 2)

EXERCISE 3

Read the following paragraph:

Of the Characters of Women clearly illustrates Pope's division of mankind. Pope, who was born in 1688, wrote this epistle in 1734. In this work, he treats the complexities of human nature and its elusiveness in the characters of women. To reinforce the theme of female inconstancy, Pope presents a variety of exempla through the skillful manipulation of a traditional literary device—the gallery of portraits.

Does this paragraph strike you as a tight, logical, straightforward discussion of a topic? It should not. An extraneous sentence flaws the presentation. Which one is it? Eliminate this sentence and then reread the paragraph. Does the topic seem to be evident and well developed after the distracting, extraneous sentence is eliminated. Check your own writing. Extraneous material should be eliminated if it is not important. If it is important enough to be discussed, it should be developed in a later paragraph. Relegate it to a footnote if it is important but does not warrant discussion. Perhaps the material itself is not extraneous, but your presentation makes it appear so. In this case, you should properly subordinate the point so that it becomes part of the development of the topic peculiar to the paragraph.

EXERCISE 4

Four possibilities are presented as conclusions to the following paragraph. While one suggestion is blatantly wrong, three are acceptable in varying degrees. Their acceptability depends on the writer's plan for the following paragraph. Choose the sentence you think to be most appropriate and be prepared to justify your choice.

It should be noted that it was the prairie writers who initiated the systematic transformation of Canadian fiction from romance to realism. One of the reasons for this transformation was the impossibility of making an idyll out of the rigorous conditions of prairie agriculture. Such conditions were hardly the background for romantic adventure. The Wild West hero who proved so hardy in American literature had little place where law and order established by the Northwest Mounted Police had preceded settlement.

1. As a result, Canadian settlers were realistic rather than romantic characters.
2. Matt Dillon was not so formidable as a Mountie.
3. The difference between American and Canadian consciousness lies in the fact that Americans are the survivors of a lawless and ugly frontier—we are not.
4. One of the prairie writers who helped initiate the movement from romance to realism is Wallace Stegner.

Read the paragraph again, concluding with the sentence of your choice. Are you happy with it? What would you argue in the next paragraph? If you do not like any of the choices provided, write your own concluding sentence and indicate why it is preferable to the options given.

EXERCISE 5

In the following paragraph, a central, transitional sentence is omitted. Three options are given as suggested transition. Choose the most suitable or create your own. Be prepared to justify your choice.

How a Canadian novel sells has often depended on how it has been reviewed, not in Toronto or Montreal newspapers, but in *The New York Times Book Review, Time,* or *The Sunday Times,* should their reviewers, in fact deign to notice. *(Choose a sentence to insert here.)*
Who would deny that our reviewers are just as competent and perceptive as foreign reviewers? Unfortunately, although the health of Canadian literature does not necessarily depend on the amount of academic scrutiny it receives, critics abroad have not always been charitable, in their smug, patronizing reviews, of even our best writers.

1. This humiliating need for the blessings of foreign critics, who have in the past ordained what is saleable and what is not, is unacceptable and is, one hopes, changing.
2. A Canadian critic is the best judge of Canadian literature, and, consequently, only he should be heeded.
3. Canadian literature should not be subjected to demeaning appraisals by critics who are not a part of the Canadian heritage.

Why did you choose the sentence you did? Read the paragraph again, supplying your transitional sentence. Has a gap in logic been filled? Avoid gaps in your own paragraphs.

A REMINDER

You have done the paragraph exercises and accepted them as such. Often a reader if faced with paragraph exercises when he or she least expects them—while reading an essay. Do not make your reader unscramble your paragraphs or provide introductions, transitions, or conclusions. If you write in a clear format, readers can elicit your content as you hope they will.

CHAPTER 3

Good Ideas Deserve Good Expression

Writing correctly and writing well are two different things. This fact is sad but true. You may possibly get to the point where your writing is grammatically flawless, but b-o-r-i-n-g, flat, and dull. While expository prose, by definition, does not allow for the same flair which creative writing involves, it should not be flatfooted and monotonous. The best way to interest your reader in your material is to write it well. Boring exposition may not keep your reader awake and alert enough to appreciate your argument. Consider your style.

TONE

There are various levels of expression. Different tones are suitable for different occasions. A wedding invitation, for instance, "cordially invites" you, while a Halloween party invitation tells you to "B.Y.O.B." Each invitation is suitable for the occasion. Similarly, a formal analysis or essay is different from a friendly letter. Contractions, slang, colloquialisms, and abbreviations are fine for the latter, but generally should be avoided in expository prose. However, do not assume that expository prose is terse and mechanical. Like creative writers, expository writers have individual styles—some good, some bad. See to it that yours is good. It must be both grammatically sound and, at the same time, clear, concise, and precise.

Interesting the reader does not mean changing your style from the formal to the frivolous. *Interesting* is not a synonym for *funny;* witty asides distract rather than engage. The purpose of expository writing is to examine and discuss an idea or ideas. In this writing, you must be convincing, but neither pompous on the one hand, nor colloquial on the other. The emphasis is on clarity; frivolity confuses and distracts. How, then, can your writing be clear and precise, and, at the same time, interesting?

VARY SENTENCE STRUCTURE

Variety in sentence structure is not a matter of chance. It is understandable, especially when you are focusing your attention on content, that you may slip into mechanically repetitive sentence structures. Consider the impact (or lack of impact) you make on a reader. Nothing is more monotonous than a series of sentences consisting of subject, verb, object; subject, verb, object *ad infinitum.* This structure is, without doubt, the safest one to use, but it can have the same effect on your reader as counting sheep. Isolated simple sentences (one subject, one verb) can be effective, but their isolation makes them so; they are merely one ingredient in an essay.

1. Length

Sentences may be varied in a number of ways. The most obvious variable is length. Complex ideas may require long, involved, and complex presentations. However, once all the complex facts in an argument are presented, the conclusion can be stated succinctly in a short, simple sentence. Thus, the reader is struck by what seems to be the simple logic of your conclusion.

2. Subordination

Just as your sentences vary in length, so too they should vary in the order of presentation of subordinate and principal material. A sentence need not necessarily start with the principal clause. Use parenthetical openers, subordinate clauses, verbal phrases, and the like to introduce some sentences. (See Chapters 9 and 10 for discussion of these subordinate constructions, if necessary.) Since variety makes your prose more readable, you will retain your reader's interest, and he or she can then concentrate on the validity of your material.

3. Intent

Most sentences in expository prose are assertive; they state facts. You may occasionally ask a question in an interrogative sentence. This *very occasional* variety in the nature of your sentences is a good stylistic technique. In general, however, avoid exclamations. They lower the register of your exposition. Variety should also be evident in the tone of your sentences. Incorporate both positive and negative statements.

4. Punctuation

Lastly, punctuate with more than merely commas and periods. (If you are not familiar with the uses of the semicolon, colon, dash, parentheses, and hyphen, see Chapter 10.) Think about places where you might use a semicolon or colon to integrate thoughts. Fuse sentences with these marks of punctuation. The *sparing use* of the dash and parentheses in internal punctuation also adds variety.

Variety is the spice of good writing. If your exposition is engaging in its presentation, it is interesting and a pleasure to read. Good ideas deserve good expression.

CONSIDER YOUR AUDIENCE

Writing is a means of communication. While analysis and discussion of a topic are rewarding to the writer, the information you impart is intended for a reader. He or she is not interested in sentimental effusions on a subject, nor in jargon-ridden technical exigeses. Do not use involved terminology which can be better expressed simply. The language of the computer room, for example, is distinct from the language of the literature class. Direct your discussions of computer programming to one audience and your literary discussions to another.

An essay is not a substitute soap box or pulpit. The literature which you are discussing is to be analyzed and assessed as *literature,* not as *morality.* Thus, your discussion should not involve "the lesson to be learned." An essay is not the place to point out, for instance, that one should learn from *King Lear* to respect one's parents. Your audience is not a congregation. Consider your audience and direct your discussion to it in a suitable tone.

DICTION

Language is your only vehicle of expression in an essay or analysis. You cannot add emphasis with hand gestures, nor can you use your voice to stress important words and points. All you have are the words on the printed page. Thus, in order for your presentation to be as strong as possible, you must use strong words and expressions.

CLICHÉS AND JARGON

Freshness and novelty in expression make for interesting sayings. However, expressions and sayings, when they are no longer fresh, lose their impact. Hackneyed expressions and clichés are trite and weak. The language in them is tired; it has been overused. Clichés make your presentation sluggish. Do I tell you much when I say that if your writing moves *at a snail's pace,* your reader will be *bored to tears* or *mad as a hornet,* and you will not be *pleased as punch* about your grade? I have used a lot of time and space to tell you that drab expression is a bore. While trying to make things *crystal clear,* I was *as clear as mud,* and made you *madder than a wet hen.* Do not distress your reader with hackneyed expressions and clichés.

Jargon, too, is unsuitable in a literary essay. *You set the parameters of your register. The matrix of your discussion is the common denominator for the cross currents of the argument. The coefficients of simultaneous arguments are averaged into a mean level of exigesis.* Have I impressed you with this jargon? Would you like some more? Of course not. Jargon is pretentious and inappropriate. Use appropriate language. If your ideas are simple-minded to begin with, no fancy-dress language will save them.

VERBS

Verbs are stronger than nouns; the former move while the latter are static. The verb *to unify,* for instance, is stronger than the phrase *to give unity; to prove* is stronger than *to provide proof.* Keep your thoughts moving on the page through the energy of verbs. If you do so, you will discover that your writing moves forward more quickly and that you use fewer words to make a point. As a result, you get the most out of your ideas and say more within your word and page limitations. You will make every word count.

STRONG VERBS

While verbs in general are stronger than nouns, verbs have a hierarchy of strength. Transitive verbs (verbs which imply action) are stronger than copulative verbs (verbs which imply a state of being). If possible, use transitive verbs. Expressions like *it is, there are,* or *there is* are seldom justified as strong openers. Get to the meat of the sentence and start there. *It is weak constructions which slow down your pace; weak expressions make your presentation sluggish.* Can you see the point? If you start strongly, adrenalin will be built up at the beginning of a statement and carry the reader through to the end.

Similarly, phrases such as *begins to, starts to,* and *seems to* plus a verb are not strong. The main verb is weakened, sometimes to the point of being ineffectual in a sentence. *When you start to use them, your sentence begins to weaken and it seems to be less strong than it should be.* Why not say that *when you use them, your sentence is weakened and less strong than it should be?* Again, time and space are issues.

VOICE

Active verbs are stronger than passive. The agent in a passive sentence must be indicated in an awkward and wordy way, while in the active voice the agent is subject. If the agent is immaterial, the passive voice may be preferred, but, if the agent is worthy of mention, he or she is less awkwardly presented in the active voice. Consider the following example:

"On First Looking into Chapman's Homer" is thought by many critics to be one of Keat's best poems.

Many critics consider "On First Looking into Chapman's Homer" one of Keats's best poems.

Which is stronger? Which is less awkward? Which do you think a reader would prefer to find in an essay? If there is no concrete reason for using the passive voice, prefer the active voice. Your presentation will be stronger and move more rapidly.

RHETORICAL DISTRIBUTION

Is it enough to agree to prefer strong verbs to weak nouns, transitive to copulative verbs, active to passive voice? Obviously, you must still use nouns, the verb *to be,* and passive constructions. What do you do with weak words and structures, since it is impossible to avoid them totally? Use them, but plan *where* to use them. Put your strength at the beginning and end of statements. Just as your essay starts and ends with strong points, so too your sentences build up momentum from the beginning and close with enough drive to carry the reader on to the next statement. If this effect is achieved, your reader will not be hindered in focusing on your content. Your presentation should then be as interesting and engaging as your material.

CONCISE EXPRESSION

One of the major reasons for flabby prose is wordiness. A point, to be assimilated easily, must be made clearly and succinctly. Clarity is generally grammatical; succinctness is a matter of good judgement. The keynote of effective prose is economy. This is not to say that necessary words and points should be omitted or that good prose is sketchy. Point and abbreviated sentence form is suitable for your outline, but not for your finished piece. Your essay is an expansion of the sketchy points in your outline. As you try to be concise, you must strike a balance between too many and too few words.

Sometimes repetition is necessary for effect; however, unnecessary repetition is wasteful and redundant. It is both an insult to your reader's intelligence and an indication of your own insecurity about your ability to make a point effectively the first time you mention it. A redundant statement says, in effect, "Maybe you didn't get this point the first time I made it, so I'll make it again." In a well planned and well written piece of prose, repetition is boring. Avoid it.

In addition to repeating a point more than is necessary, some writers often use too many words to make a point. Consider the following sentence:

It is Satan who orders the building of Hell, Pandemonium, after the angels have fallen, have rebelled against God.

First of all, *it is . . . who* is wordy and unnecessary. Must this writer use both *Hell* and *Pandemonium* to label the fallen angels' abode? Is it necessary to explain *fallen* in this sentence? Rewrite the sentence.

Satan orders the fallen angels to build Pandemonium after their rebellion against God.

This example is more concise while still providing all the necessary information.

Remember that conciseness and shortness are two different things. Something that is concise is free of redundancies and extra words. A concise piece of writing may, in fact, be very long. In it, however, every word is there for a reason. It has been said that brevity is the soul of wit. As you work on your essay, remember that conciseness is the soul of good writing. Write economically.

The following is a sample list of expressions which should be used sparingly or not at all in an essay writer's vocabulary.

It is . . . who
very . . . (If you need very [or extremely] to accentuate a word, find a stronger word. For example, change very angry to furious.)
definitely . . .
. . . being + adjective (Put the adjective before the someone or something. Change, for instance, the rain being heavy, to heavy rain.)
serves to illustrate
It is clear that . . .
the fact that
noun which is adjective (Again, use the adjective before the noun. Change pride which is strong to strong pride, for example.)
the aspect of

Add to this list. Find your own repetitive and extraneous expressions. Every writer has them. The good writer is aware of his or hers, and uses them only when they are necessary for clarity.

PRECISE EXPRESSION

Not only must your writing be concise, but also it must be precise. You must be sure that your reader knows exactly what you mean by the words you use. Many words have various shades of meaning. The context of a word dictates which shade of meaning should be attributed to it in a particular instance. Using the wrong word in the wrong context often produces ludicrous results. These "bloopers" make you look inept and detract from your credibility. Consider the following "blooper":

In this book, the leaders are exposed throughout the war.

This writer has told you that, throughout the war, the leaders were without trousers. That is unlikely. The statement is ridiculous. What should be exposed?

In this book, the author exposes the motives of the leaders throughout the war.

Here the *motives,* rather than the *leaders* themselves, are exposed. This is what the writer probably meant to imply.

See that every word you use is suitable within its context. Do not set traps for yourself by experimenting with new and unfamiliar vocabulary in a formal piece of writing. Be comfortable with an expression before you present it to a reader. By all means, expand your vocabulary, but use it formally only when you are able to use it correctly.

The thesaurus is an invaluable tool in finding new vocabulary. In it you find synonyms and antonyms, and, by using these words, you eliminate excessive repetition in your writing. However, the fact that one word is a synonym for another does not necessarily mean that both words are used in the same context. For example, the words may be synonyms, but they may be followed by different prepositions. Sometimes a word may change meaning according to its complement in a phrase. For example, you can be *concerned with, in,* or *about. Concern* takes on different shades of meaning as it is complemented by different prepositions.

Use a thesaurus to expand your vocabulary. However, after you have found a word in the thesaurus, check the dictionary to discover how it is used.

PRECISE VERB TENSES

You know that since verbs are strong, action words, they are the driving force in your writing. A good writer prefers verbs to nouns, and strong to weak verbs, to add force to an argument. However, verbs often present problems to writers. You must be precise and consistent in the tenses of your verbs.

In literary essays the usual tense is the *historical present.* There is a very good reason for this convention. Something that is printed exists. At the time when an author, playwright, or poet puts words in a character's mouth, the character speaks. The character continues to utter these words each time the literary work is read. For example, Shakespeare wrote *Romeo and Juliet* in the 1590's. When he wrote the play, Juliet said, "O Romeo, Romeo! wherefore art thou Romeo?" However, the play is produced all over the world, and Juliet comes on stage and *says,* "O Romeo, Romeo! wherefore art thou Romeo?" Every time someone reads the play she says it. She *says* (not *said*) it when you quote her in an essay. Like all published material, Juliet's words exist in the historical present tense.

The general use of the historical present tense does not imply that you never use past, future, or perfect tenses in your essays. Each verb you use should be in a tense appropriate to its context. There may be an excuse for switching tenses midstream, but this must be a valid excuse, not just a whim or the writer's part. Be precise. Consider the following passage:

Milton wanted to have written the great English epic. He begins to write an Arthuriad but changed his plans. Paradise Lost was originally intended to be a tragedy, but it will be an epic instead.

Do you feel at sea in this maze of verb tenses? You should. Where in time is the writer focusing his or her attention? He or she has included present, past, future, and perfect tenses. How would you correct it? Consider the principal tense and justify all departures from it.

Milton wanted to write the great English epic. He began to write an Arthuriad but changed his plans. Paradise Lost was originally intended to be a tragedy, but it is an epic instead.

This selection is written principally in the past tense because it focuses on past action. A perfect infinitive *(to have written)* is changed to a simple complementary infinitive *(to write)* in the first sentence. The final verb, *is,* is in the present tense because it refers to a piece of writing that *exists* in an eternal, historical, present tense—*Paradise Lost.*

Slipping tenses is easy to do. Exert some control over your verbs; they are strong words and may get away from you.

Be consistent, precise, and concise in your writing. If you have something worth writing and write it well, success will follow.

EXERCISE 1

Each of the following sentences has problems in register, concision, or precision. Rewrite each sentence, correcting the problems. Remember, you are considering these sentences as formal expository prose.

1. Time is frozen on the Grecian urn, just as the young man is on the verge of the maiden.

   _____

   _____

2. There are several reasons why this poem was an ode and not a sonnet.

   _____

   _____

3. By the time Pip grew up, his movement from innocence to experience is complete.

   _____

   _____

4. During the time when Mary Shelley is writing *Frankenstein* the Gothic novel is popular.

   _____

   _____

5. Emma Bovary had a future and a behind.

   _____

   _____

6. It is plain to see that this book is equally as interesting as his earlier works.

   _____

   _____

7. It was at dusk, at 5 A.M. in the morning, when the story opens.

   _____

   _____

8. This play is written in the year 1846.

_____

_____

9. Morag Gunn is no live wire; she would never be the life of the party.

_____

_____

10. Emma Bovary's is one of the most antagonizing of deaths possible.

_____

_____

11. The moral is clear from the offset; there is no room for doubt about what the poet is trying to say.

_____

_____

12. Therefore, in conclusion, it might be said that all that glitters is not gold.

_____

_____

13. Hence, as a result, good prevails.

_____

_____

14. When Lear appeared on the heath, he is clearly as crazy as a loon.

_____

_____

15. No one, not a single person, has the foggiest idea why he acts this way.

_____

_____

16. It is at noon, 12 P.M., when Satan tempts Eve in the garden as she is tending her crops, performing her agricultural duties.

_____

_____

17. Unfortunately, his last work was never completed; he died before he has time to have finished it.

_____

_____

18. Leggatt was the *alter ego* of the captain; he is his other self.

_____

_____

19. Since the author was born in 1887, he will be 28 when he wrote this piece.

_____

_____

20. No one moves; time is frozen; all is still; the action stops.

_____

_____

21. It is in chapter VI that the action begins to speed up and the characters seem to come alive.

_____

_____

22. It has been decided by the foremost critics that this is his weakest novel.

_____

_____

23. Because of the fact that he uses the stream of consciousness he could be said to be a follower of Joyce.

_____

_____

24. It is Tristram Shandy himself, being very introspective, who makes this realization.

_____

_____

25. Through the use of the metaphor of the circle, the unity has been achieved.

_____

_____

EXERCISE 2

Consider the following sentences. Can you determine the error or errors in each? Rewrite the sentences. Justify your revisions. Use your dictionary if you have to.

1. They did not marry for love; there's was a marriage of convenients.

_____

_____

2. In the novel, *The Stone Angel,* the authoress, Margaret Laurence, discussed her heroine, Hagar Shipley, geriatrically.

_____

_____

3. Jim is the character that contributes immensely to Huck's maturity.

_____

_____

4. The climax in this tale is when Gawain and the Green Knight encounter, meet, come face-to-face.

_____

_____

5. The responsibility is distributed between Adam, Eve, and Satan.

_____

_____

6. On the one hand, *Gulliver's Travels* is ironic; on the other hand, it is satiric; on the other hand, it is scatalogical.

_____

_____

7. The satire begins to mount as Gulliver starts to address the king satirically.

_____

_____

8. Due to the fact that this tale does not begin at the beginning, it might be said to be *in medias res*.

_____

_____

9. As well as having a moral, the novel furthermore has an interesting plot.

_____

_____

10. The characters of the pilgrims can be said to emerge as Chaucer characterized them in terms of social rank, dress, and language.

_____

_____

11. Therefore, in conclusion, we might say that Donne is a metaphysical poet in every sense of the word.

_____

_____

12. The principle characters participate in one plot; the minor characters perform the sub-plot.

_____

_____

13. *Robinson Crusoe* is an early example of the form of journalism; it is written in the form of a diary.

_____

_____

14. Whereas this poem is a sonnet, it has fourteen lines.

_____

_____

15. "The Canonization" is the poem where Donne uses the sacred to refer to the secular.

_____

_____

16. Ulysses returns home and faced an unanticipated battle.

_____

_____

17. It is the houses where characters live which provide insight into the values of the people who live there.

_____

_____

18. If this play had less minor characters, it would be easier to follow.

_____

_____

19. Once the action started, the tension began to build, and the affect is one of intensity.

_____

_____

20. This story is set in a setting of green.

_____

_____

21. This critic seems to be interested only in the allegory; he is disinterested by everything else.

_____

_____

22. In the beginning, Hotspur is in favour and Hal is in disfavour; they end oppositely.

_____

_____

23. A difference is evident in their approaches, attitudes, and opinions towards marriage.

_____

_____

24. In "The Wasteland," T.S. Eliot uses both classical and biblical illusions.

_____

_____

25. Thus, one might conclude that the function of the house might be to symbolize the inhabitant.

_____

_____

CHAPTER 4

Editing, Revising, and Rewriting

Writers often have to face the "blank page syndrome" when they are faced with assignments. You have ten or fifteen blank pages; they must be filled with good expository prose. What do you do? You have a lot to say (if you have done your organizational work), but how do you say it? The obvious place to start is at the beginning; you know you should write an appropriate introduction, but you cannot seem to get started.

The solution to this problem is logical. With outline in hand, begin to work on your first draft. If the introduction intimidates you, skip it for now and work on the body of the essay. Bear in mind that this is your *first,* and not your *final* draft. Get something down on paper; it does not have to be great—yet. Allow room for revisions in your written draft. Double space your writing. If every line and word is crowded together, you will not be able to edit your work effectively. Work through the body of the assignment and then attack the introduction and conclusion.

You will find that, once you get started with your writing, it will become progressively easier. You must get your material down on paper; you can work on polishing your presentation in the next draft or drafts. The important thing to remember is that your first draft is for *you,* not for your reader. Very few people can write a flawless first draft. Mistakes are forgivable at this stage of writing, so long as you correct them in later drafts.

When your first draft is done, consider it objectively. Read it aloud and note the awkward sections. Focus on presentation, grammar, and syntax rather than on content in a first reading. Consider content separately in the next reading. Are you sure you have said everything you want to say? Do your arguments follow your outline? Have you linked your thoughts? Work through the draft with a different coloured ink. Put yourself in the place of your reader and then make the corrections you think he or she would like to see. Transpose sentences; vary their lengths; check for conciseness and preciseness.

The following is the first draft of the introduction of an essay on Donne's death imagery. Like all first drafts, it needs revisions. Read it aloud and then make corrections. Mark up the draft in preparation for rewriting it.

NOTE: The parenthetical reference in the text refers to a book which would be listed in a "Works Cited" list at the end of the essay. The appropriate bibliographic entry for the work in the Works Cited is given at the end of the draft.

That John Donne, the man, was very much obsessed with the concept of death and mortality is apparent in the works of John Donne, the poet. For him, death was a phenomenon to be held constantly before one's eyes and contemplated in a variety of contexts. Introspection with emphasis on death gave rise to conflict as Donne tried to affirm his worthiness and at the same time overcome his sense of unworthiness while attempting to compensate for the anxiety and isolation which gave rise to a conflict and tension between body and soul. Donne's certainty of salvation was replaced by a feeling of nothingness. Thus death was considered attainment of the sublime. Also something to be feared. Assurance of God's mercy was replaced by the problems of: beauty and goodness versus evil, man's free will versus predestination. Thus, paradox was the result of Donne's attempt to reconcile himself about the reality of death. It is from Donne's poetic imagery of death that there issues, "that sense of man's mortality, decay ever-present, and the skull beneath the skin" (Rugoff 234).

However, Donne's attitude toward death is not stable. The paradox surrounding the concept of mortality in the mind of Donne results in a spectrum of attitudes toward death. In his early poems Donne can exercise his wit, punning and placing death on the same level as orgasm and sleep, death is expanded in later poems to be synonomous with separation, ecstasy, and, at times, even the end of life. Donne's mature poems view death as something which each man must come to terms with, either in fear and trembling, or as a triumphant victor through the mercy of a godhead. Thus, as Donne matures, as his dealings with the concept of death become more direct, the spectrum of attitudes widens, and death is treated as a reality. A direct consideration of Donne's poetry will establish that the spectrum exists.

WORK CITED

Rugoff, Milton Allen. *Donne's Imagery: A Study in Creative Sources.* New York: Russell & Russell, 1962.

Compare your corrections with the example which follows:

(That) John Donne, (the man) was (very much) obsessed with the concept of death and
His poetry indicates this.   *Donne*
mortality, ~~is apparent in the works of John Donne, the poet.~~ For ~~him,~~ death was a phenomenon to be held constantly before one's eyes and contemplated in a variety of
                    too wordy
contexts. [Introspection with emphasis on death gave rise to conflict as Donne tried to affirm his worthiness and, at the same time, overcome his sense of unworthiness, ~~while~~
the resulting   *culminates in*
~~attempting to compensate for the~~ anxiety and isolation which ~~gave rise to~~ a (conflict and)
                                     original   *is*
tension between body and soul.] Donne's certainty of salvation ~~was~~ replaced by a feeling
              Donne considers death   *,but also*
of nothingness. (Thus) death was considered attainment of the sublime, [~~Also~~ something
              Complacency about   *is*   *tensions between*
to be feared.] ~~Assurance of~~ God's mercy ~~was~~ replaced by the (problems of) beauty and   *frag.*
          and   *and*   *Donne's attempt*
goodness ~~versus~~ evil; man's free will ~~versus~~ predestination. (Thus) paradox was the result
                                                    result in paradox:
of Donne's attempt) to reconcile himself about the reality of death. ~~It is~~ From Donne's poetic imagery ~~of death~~ (that there) issues "that sense of man's mortality, decay ever-present, and the skull beneath the skin" (Rugoff 234).

However, Donne's attitude toward death is not stable. The paradox ~~surrounding~~ *inherent in* the concept of mortality (in the mind of Donne) results in a spectrum of attitudes toward death. In his early poems ~~Donne~~ *Donne's* (can) exercise *he* his wit, punning and placing death on the same level as orgasm and sleep; *Death* death is expanded in later poems to be synonomous *sp* with separation, ecstasy, and, at times, even the end of life. Donne's ~~mature~~ *later* poems view death as something which *with* each man must come to terms with, either in fear and trembling, or as a triumphant victor through ~~the mercy of a godhead~~ *divine mercy* (Thus,) as Donne matures, (as)

thus 3

his dealings with the concept of death become more direct; the spectrum of attitudes widens; and death is treated as a reality. ~~A direct consideration of Donne's poetry will establish that the spectrum exists.~~

WORK CITED

Rugoff, Milton Allen. *Donne's Imagery: A Study in Creative Sources.* New York: Russell & Russell, 1962.

Can you see the degree to which a first draft might be improved?

The writer of the Donne essay has started out lamely. The essay must have a more definite and aggressive tone. The opening of an essay cannot be sluggish. The opening in question must move more quickly. Thus, the involved first sentence is changed to two strong sentences. The third sentence is seemingly endless with a series of tags at the end. It must be divided into smaller parts, and those parts must be tightened. The following sentences are more manageable in regard to the amount of material in each, but they still need editing and revision.

This writer has problems with verb tenses. Donne's poetry exists in the historical present tense; consequently, while Donne himself *was* and *thought,* his poetry *is.* As the essay continues, the verb *to be* is overused, and, as a result, the writing weakens. For example, *was the result* is weaker than *resulted.*

Punctuation must be considered. The unforgiveable (in a final draft) errors of sentence fragment and comma splice *must* be corrected. Misuse of comma and colon is evident and marked.

Transitions are crucial in tight, logical exposition. This writer repeatedly uses *thus* as a catch-all transition. He or she must consider other transitional techniques.

Every piece of writing can be improved. Each should be improved to grammatical perfection and, one hopes, to a more engaging style. Consider the rewritten piece:

> John Donne was obsessed with the concept of death and mortality. The writings of the poet indicate the concerns of the man. For Donne, death was a phenomenon to be held constantly before every man's eyes and to be contemplated in a variety of contexts. Introspection focusing on death creates conflict as Donne tries to affirm his worthiness and, at the same time, overcome his sense of unworthiness. The resulting anxiety and isolation reflect a tension between body and soul. Donne's original certainty of salvation is replaced by a feeling of nothingness. As a result of this feeling, Donne considers death something to be feared. His initial optimism wanes. Complacency about God's mercy is replaced by the tension between beauty and goodness and evil, between man's free will and predestination. Thus, Donne's attempts to reconcile himself to the reality of death create a paradox. From Donne's poetic imagery issues "that sense of man's mortality, decay everpresent, and the skull beneath the skin." (Rugoff 234).

> However, Donne's attitude toward death is not stable. The paradox inherent in the concept of mortality results in a spectrum of attitudes toward death. In Donne's early poems he exercises his wit, punning, and placing death on the same level as orgasm and sleep. Death is expanded in later poems to be synonymous with separation, ecstasy, and, at times, the end of life. Donne's later poems view death as something with which each man must come to terms, either in fear and trembling or as a triumphant victor through divine mercy. As Donne matures, his dealings with the concept of death become more direct; the spectrum of attitudes widens, and death is treated as a reality.

WORK CITED

Rugoff, Milton, Allen. *Donne's Imagery: A Study in Creative Sources.* New York: Russell & Russell, 1962.

While the first draft says nothing substantially different from the second, the first is stylistically inferior.

Never submit a first draft. Allow yourself time to apply the stylistic techniques you have perfected and both you and your reader should be satisfied with the work you submit.

PART II

The Research Paper

CHAPTER 5

Library Research

When you are assigned to write a research paper, *writing* is only half your job. You have to search for material in general and then search again (re-search) among your general material for points which apply to your particular area. While in a literary *essay* you are concerned almost exclusively with literary works (primary sources), in a research paper you must analyze evaluations, critiques, analyses, and reviews of the literature which have been done by others (secondary sources). Your research brings you in contact with professional criticism that has been done on your topic; your organization and writing of the research paper consolidates what has been written on your topic, and one hopes, adds credence to your own evaluation of the literature in question. The task is formidable and even intimidating. Your responsibility lies in making the task manageable and then completing it.

DEFINING THE TASK

Your research assignment will, of course, bring you to the library. However, preparatory thinking and planning precede your library research. You are dealing with both *primary* and *secondary* sources; by definition, your primary sources come first. In other words, you must read and think about the literary work with which you are dealing before evaluating what critics have written about the writer and the work in question. Not only must you know the primary material, but also you must decide what aspect of the literature you will consider. As in any essay, you have to decide on a topic, after reading the primary material, and then narrow your topic. In so doing, you will be moving from an impossible to a possible amount of research. It is impossible, for example, to find and read everything in the library on Alexander Pope; however, you should be able to find a reasonable amount of material on the function of the card game in *The Rape of the Lock*. You can make your task reasonable, or you can be your own worst enemy. The decision is yours.

FINDING RESEARCH MATERIAL

The time has come for a trip to the library. While you should be able to make some headway on your own, it is important to remember that help is available. Reference librarians are helpful people, but they cannot help you unless you request their assistance. If the library is a maze to you, sign up for a library tour so you will have some idea of the building's physical plan and resources. If, after a tour, you are still uncertain about where and how to look for material, ask for help.

The first items that come to mind in terms of research material are books. How do you find books that the library has on your topic? Search in the card or micro-catalogue before wandering in the stacks. The material in the catalogues is organized in files: author and title (separate or combined) and subject files. Some libraries have on-line computer terminals which will identify material available in files of author names, titles, and subjects.

For example, you might find works on *The Rape of the Lock* under Pope, the title, or under eighteenth century poetry. While knowing where to look in the author and title files may be no problem for you, you may find the subject file an enigma *unless* you know what subjects you should consider.

Your problem can be solved if you check the *Library of Congress List of Subject Headings,* a book located near the subject catalogue. Here you will find such subjects as "feminine influence in literature," "extemporaneous speaking," and "folk literature." When you find a suitable subject heading for your topic, you will be able to determine what books the library has on that topic. At this point, you can go to the stacks and locate any books which seem suitable for your research.

PREVIEWING BOOKS

A book may *seem* suitable and, in fact, be of no use to you in your research. Remember the old adage: "You can't judge a book by its cover." Similarly, you can't judge a book by its title, author, or subject heading. Once you have a book in hand, you must preview it to determine whether all, or part of it may be useful to you. Of course, the title may give you *some* indication, as may the author. Who is the critic? Is he or she noted for any particular critical bias? What does the critic say in the preface? Why was the book written—to propose new critical interpretations?—to refute an accepted critical opinion?—to emphasize new points? The critic should indicate the genesis of his or her book in the preface. The preface is not something to be skipped; reading it may induce you to skip reading a book which is not useful to you at this time or encourage you to consider a book carefully.

Check also the table of contents to get an idea of the book's scope. How much emphasis is placed on your topic? You do not have to read every book cover to cover as you do your research. You do not have the time. Determine from the table of contents how much of a book is useful to you *at this time*. Likewise, check the index. Again, you may be able to determine how useful the book may be for your particular topic.

After you have previewed all the books which you had anticipated might be useful, you will have selected the most suitable works. These are the books you consider as you research and from which you take notes.

ARTICLES AND REVIEWS

Books are only one of many sources for research. They are, in fact, the most cumbersome research tools. You will find that articles and book reviews are less unwieldy, more succinct, and generally more recent. However, tracking down useful articles involves detective skills intimidating to many students. Be logical and methodical in looking for research material; short cuts usually lead to dead ends.

Individual articles and reviews are never published independently; they appear in periodicals and journals. How do you know that a journal has an article which might interest you? Browsing in the stacks of the periodicals room will not help. Do you flip through the table of contents of every journal in hopes of finding something on your topic? You can do so if you want, but it is not necessary. The search through journals and periodicals has already been done for you. Use the resources available in the reference area of the periodicals section of the library.

Important reference tools are the following:

1. *Periodical Indices.* Indices of non-book materials *by subject.* These are published monthly and bound yearly. Articles from hundreds of periodicals are indexed. Some also include reference to book reviews.
2. *Abstracts.* Indices of book and non-book materials. These include summaries of the works mentioned.
3. *Book Review Index* and *Book Review Digest.* Indices of book reviews, organized by the books' approximate publication dates.
4. *Essay and General Literature Index.* Indices by *author* and *subject.* Reference is made to essays and articles in collections and anthologies.
5. *Newspaper Indices.* Possible sources for theatre and book reviews. These indices include the *New York Times Index* and the *Canadian Newspaper Index.*

Indices such as those mentioned here eliminate much of the footwork in searching for research material. Once you have found references to articles which you would like to consider, find the correct volume of the journal or periodical, and you are on your way to finding material for your research paper.

NOTE TAKING

After finding research materials, you must read and think about them. However, another activity is integrated with your reading and thinking process at this point; note taking is crucial to research. Do not expect to remember points which strike you as you read secondary material. In fact, do not expect to remember anything. Take notes; take adequate notes. If you take too many notes, you can eliminate some; if you take too few notes, you are in trouble. Accumulate notes which you think may be relevant to your research; if you do not need a particular note when you actually write your paper, you can discard it then. *Do not* however, copy pages and pages of a book or article. Condense, paraphrase, abbreviate. Be able, however, to attribute every note to its source.

Each researcher perfects his or her own system of note taking. Like an outline, notes are for *your* use as a writer. Take notes which you, as a writer, can use. The most endorsed and perhaps the best practice is to take notes on index cards; notes taken on cards are manageable, and most easily sorted, organized, shuffled, and reshuffled into a coherent pattern. A note should be taken for each idea that may work into a different part of your paper. "Note," in this case, implies an individual card (or 3″ × 5″ piece of paper).

To save yourself time, effort, and ink, you should make up a *complete* bibliography card for each book, article, or review from which you are taking notes. For instance, for a collection of articles, make up a card for each article you will use. See the example which follows:

Scott, Evelyn. "On William Faulkner's
The Sound and the Fury."
Twentieth Century Interpretations
of The Sound and the Fury.
Ed. Michael H. Cowan. Englewood
Cliffs: Prentice, 1968. 26-7.

Making full bibliographic entries at this point will save frustration when you are typing the bibliography of your finished research paper. Merely put the bibliography cards of the works which you have cited in alphabetical order, and type from the cards.

Full bibliography cards will also save references on note cards. A sample form of a note card might be the following: at the top, an identifying phrase; in the center, the note (a quotation, paraphrase, summary, or factual statement); at the bottom the reference (author, shortened title,

Characterization - S.&F

[Jason is a devil caught in a world of] "petty, sadistic lunacy."

Compson family - reflected in Yoknapatawpha County.

Scott, pp. 26-27.

if necessary, and page). Use quotation marks in your notes for *verbatim* citations. In quotations, use the spelling of your source, and be scrupulous in copying a direct quotation exactly. Insert your own statements within a quotation in brackets.

Once you have taken all your notes, you can sort through them, arranging them in categories and considering a potential pattern for the outline of your research paper. Discard redundant notes; see where your research has led you; plan your paper. After organizing your material in outline form, you can begin your assignment as it was phrased: you can "write a research paper," using the fruits of your research to validate and substantiate your development of a thesis.

CHAPTER 6

Quotations and Source Acknowledgment

As you write essays, analyses, and research papers, *your* arguments, and *your* expression of those arguments are the crucial factors. Reference to primary and secondary materials lends credence to your arguments. It is impossible to develop a thesis without reference to primary sources at least, and, in a research paper, you must cite both primary and secondary sources.

Different faculties and departments prefer different citation formulae. Suitable style sheets for English papers are the following: Wiles' *Scholarly Reporting in the Humanities, The M.L.A. Style Sheet,* and Turabian's *A Manual for Writers.* It is important for you to establish which style of documentation you are required to use, then use it *consistently.* The examples and discussions in this chapter adhere to recommendations in the 1984 *MLA Handbook for Writers of Research Papers.*

Your writing style is your own. In writing, as in everything else, practice makes perfect. As you continue to write, your style develops and is consistent throughout any given piece of writing. However, when you back up what you say with references to primary or secondary sources, you are using a writer or critic's style within your explication. This merging of styles leads to a major problem area in expository writing—the question of quotations and source acknowledgment.

PLAGIARISM

You cannot "steal" another person's ideas or expressions. This form of theft is plagiarism and is grounds for failure in, if not expulsion from, a course. There is, of course, a difference between intended and inadvertent plagiarism. Quote, cite, acknowledge when you present work which is not your own. The offense of plagiarism is serious, but it can be avoided by acknowledging or citing the source of your material. In this case, you "borrow," but do not "steal" someone's work.

Attempts to avoid plagiarism sometimes lead to a new problem—over-acknowledging or over-citing. You are a student; you cannot be expected to have the scope of knowledge that professionals in the field of literature have. Since you are a student and do not have literary definitions, critical terms, or chronology at the tip of your fingers, you will have to look up and learn many facts which you will subsequently use in your writing. *All* this material need not be acknowledged because it is not necessary to footnote material that is "in the common realm." As a general rule, material which appears in a number of sources—say three—belongs to everyone. For example, you may have to look up the publication date of a work with which you are dealing. You do not know the date yourself, so it is not actually your own material. On the other hand, probably dozens of people have mentioned the publication date in their published works. You need not acknowledge your source. Similarly, material in your instructor's lectures is *gratis*. You may use as your own any lecture material since it was *given* to you. Do not footnote the lecturer, but avoid merely rehashing lecture notes in your essay or research paper.

QUOTATIONS

Quotations serve the purpose of elucidating; thus, they should not confuse. Unfortunately, many students produce "sore thumbs" when quoting. You have your own style. So too, authors, playwrights, poets, and critics have individual styles. When you quote one of them directly, you face the potential problem of mis-matched syntax. Unless you skillfully work a quotation into your exposition, your presentation will be uneven. Rare is the student who has developed a good quotation technique. You may be surprised to learn, however, that perceptive quotation is often the difference between a good essay and a truly excellent one.

Many students seem to use quotations as padding. They theorize that the more words they quote, the fewer original words they need. This theory is not valid. A plethora of unnecessary quotations confuses and irritates. Quotations properly used, however, are an excellent way to signal your personal insight into a work of literature, or to show how a sweeping generalization applies to a work in detail. Quotations have different purposes: some merely present and introduce a passage to be discussed; others illustrate a general statement; others, the most subtle, capture verbal nuances that would be destroyed by paraphrase. Each kind is indispensible to the writer.

In order to fuse your presentation with the material being cited, you must not quote abruptly. Prepare your reader for a quotation; quote; indicate the impact of the quotation. Determine the purpose of a particular quotation, then present it in such a way that it will function appropriately. If there is a grammatical or stylistic discrepancy between your presentation and a quotation, the result will be confusion. Since your aim should be clarity, this confusion must be avoided. Introduce a quotation with your own words and the correct punctuation. Make adjustments in the quoted material in brackets. Watch particularly for verb tense consistency and appropriate pronoun reference.

If the quotation cannot stand independently, it must be linked grammatically to the rest of your text. Quote as much as necessary and punctuate the sentence as if the quotation marks were not there. Consider the following example:

She was attracted to Sir Lancelot "his dark bouncing curls."

Sir Lancelot's "dark bouncing curls" attracted the lady.

"His dark bouncing curls" serve no grammatical function in the first, incorrect sentence, while they are the subject of the corrected version. Most errors in quoting arise because the quotation fails to make grammatical sense with the rest of the sentence. Remember, your sentence must make sense with or without the quotation marks.

LENGTH OF QUOTATIONS

The length of a quotation depends on the circumstances: it may be longer than a page, or as short as a single word. The single general rule is to quote only as much as necessary, *and no more*. The longer the quotation, the greater the weight of comment relating to it.

1. Prose Quotations

A short quotation is included as part of the text; it is set off with quotation marks and is double spaced, like the rest of the text.

> *Mademoiselle de Bechette's routine never alters. The days "[tick] on like the mechanism of a good Swiss watch" (Hebert "House" 78).*

The original quotation was "The programme of the day was ticking on like the mechanism of a good Swiss watch." The writer has altered the tense and selected the portion of the original quotation which is suitable in his or her discussion.

A long quotation is double spaced and indented ten spaces from the left margin. Thus, if you are quoting four or more full typed lines, you set the quotation off in a single spaced block. When you do this, quotation marks are superfluous. If you use quotation marks *and* indent, you have said "Quote" twice. This repetition is not necessary.

> *Madame de Vionnet speaks of her plans for her daughter:*
>
> > *My great desire is to give my daughter the opportunity of making [Mamie's]*
> >
> > *acquaintance. I'm always on the lookout for such chances for her (James*
> >
> > *Ambassadors 260)*

The indentation indicates a quotation; thus, quotation marks are absent.

Notice the punctuation surrounding a quotation. If a full sentence quotation is introduced by a complete sentence, a colon precedes the quotation. Punctuation of short quotations and parts of sentences subscribes to the rule within the particular sentence. (See Chapter 10 for punctuation rules.)

2. Poetry Quotations

Poetry quotations are often problematical. While lines of prose are arbitrary in duration, lines of poetry are defined and regulated *as lines*. You, in quoting poetry, cannot tamper with lines and line lengths. Like short prose quotations, short poetry quotations (three lines or fewer) are double spaced and grammatically integrated in your work. Yet, you must keep the lines intact. A quoted line of poetry ends with the appropriate punctuation provided by the poet and a slash (/). You need a space before and after the slash. The beginning of the next line is capitalized if it is capitalized in the original source. As in prose quotations, you must prepare the reader for the quotation and punctuate appropriately.

> *Originally Faustus treats damnation lightly: "This word damnation terrifies not me / Nor I confound Hell in Elisium" (Marlowe Faustus I.iii.55–56).*

Since, in poetry, you are quoting *lines,* your reference is to act, scene, and *line* in poetic drama; book and *line* in epic poetry; and *line* in a poem. Page numbers are much less helpful in locating a source; do not use them.

Long poetry quotations are double spaced and indented ten spaces from the left margin. Follow the poet's line determination; within the quotation, punctuate as the poet has; introduce the quotation appropriately.

> *The epic boast appears with regularity throughout Marlowe's* Tamburlaine: Part I. *However, while Tamburlaine utters boasts, they do not conform to the epic tradition. Tamburlaine's boasts are not premature foreshadows of defeat; his boasts ring true:*

> *I hold the fates found fast in iron chains,*
>
> *And with my hand turn Fortune's wheel about;*
>
> *And sooner shall the sun fall from his sphere*
>
> *Than Tamburlaine be slain or overcome (I.ii.174–77)*

Again, quotation marks are not necessary in this indented quotation.

POINTS TO REMEMBER

Keep the following points in mind and your manner of quoting will be lucid.

1. Be sure that a fragmentary quotation links grammatically with your sentence.
2. Be sure that no unnecessary punctuation intrudes between the fragmentary quotation and the rest of your text. Remember, punctuate just as you would if the quotation marks were not there.
3. Be sure that a quoted independent sentence is signalled by a colon if your introduction is a complete sentence. Do *not* use a semicolon in this instance.
4. Be sure that the quotation following the colon is *in fact* an independent sentence.
5. *Never* allow your sentence to "straddle" a long quotation. The result may look reasonable to the eye, but it confuses the ear. Consider the following:

   Celia tries to disuade Volpone. However, her retort about her innocence which

   Is all I can think wealthy, or worth enjoying, And which, once lost, I have naught to lose beyond it, Cannot be taken by these sensual baits (III.vii.206–8),
   is distant and bland. Her pale response is not strong.

   Is the reader apt to follow that the *retort* is distant and bland? The quotation interrupts rather than augments the argument.
6. Use single quotation marks to indicate a quotation within a quotation.
7. Use brackets, not parentheses, to add your own words to a quotation.
8. Ellipses (. . .) indicate that words have been omitted in a quotation. Use them *internally* in or *after* a fragmentary quotation, not *before* the quoted material.

PARAPHRASING

If you can express a point, inference, or interpretation in your own words without distorting the writer's original meaning, do so. To alleviate the problem of mis-matched syntax and style, you might paraphrase rather than quote directly. Thus, you will present another person's ideas in your own words and style. You cite the source, but do not use quotation marks.

Never quote merely to fill space. Integrate citations with your discussion. Prefer short quotations to long ones. As a rule, the longer the quotation, the more detailed analysis it demands. Quote an outside source *verbatim* only if a point is made much more clearly than you could make it if you paraphrased. *Never do both:* a paraphrase of a quotation is redundant. Do not plagiarize on the one hand; but do not over-quote on the other. Your work should be an indication of your ideas, backed up by outside sources when necessary; your assignment in an essay or research paper is *not* to produce an anthology of what anyone has ever said or written about your topic.

SOURCE ACKNOWLEDGMENT

You must indicate the sources of all your quotations or paraphrases. Your list of Works Cited, at the end of your essay or research paper, provides full documentation of the books, articles, and other sources which you have consulted. Brief parenthetical citations within your paper supply abbreviated bibliographical material and page references. They refer the reader to the Works Cited page of your paper.

FORMAL FOOTNOTES

It is not necessary to use formal footnotes to cite references. You refer to works you quote or paraphrase in parenthetical notations. You may use a footnote if, indeed, you need to supply an informational note. If you provide additional information which is really parenthetical to the discussion in your paper, you provide this information in a footnote. However, such notes are seldom required in standard undergraduate research papers.

If, however, you find you need such notations, they should be numbered consecutively throughout your work. Your first footnote is [1], followed by [2,3,4] and so on. Notice the number is raised one half line. It *follows* the material requiring discussion in the note. Your footnote (at the foot of a page) or endnote (in a page at the end of the paper) numbers correspond to these raised numerals.

PARENTHETICAL CITATIONS (INFORMAL FOOTNOTES)

Sources of quotations or paraphrases are cited parenthetically within your paper. Generally, you need mention only an author's name and the page(s) from which you have taken material. The citation follows the material you have quoted or paraphrased, and the punctuation at the end of the sentence follows the parenthetical reference.

Bilbo names his sword: "I will give you a name, . . . and I shall call you *Sting*" (Tolkein 144).

If, however, the author of the work you cite is mentioned in your text, you need not supply his or her name in the parenthetical reference; in this case, a reference to a page number or numbers is sufficient.

Tolkein describes Smaug as "an immeasurable bat" (197).

The reader will find a full reference to the Tolkein work in the Works Cited as follows:

Tolkein, J·R·R· *The Hobbit.* London: Unwin, 1966.

Sometimes you refer to more than a single work by an author in your research paper. If you must differentiate between or among more than one book by Tolkein, for example, you provide the following: author's name, abbreviated title of the work, and page number(s).

Treebeard warns that the water will be foul "until all the filth of Saruman is washed away" (Tolkein *Two Towers* 217).

The reader will expect to find more than one reference to Tolkein's work in the Works Cited.

WORKS CITED

Tolkein, J·R·R· *The Hobbit*. London: Unwin, 1966.

————. *The Two Towers*. London: Unwin, 1982.

BIBLIOGRAPHY (Or Works Cited)

While you mention sources as they occur in your text, the bibliography is ordered alphabetically. Fuller documentation is provided in the bibliography than in the notes. Complete information on sources is included in the bibliography.

Generally, only the works cited in your essay or research paper are included in the bibliography. If, however, you found useful and pertinent information in your research, but did not cite the source in your paper, you *may* include this work in your bibliography. Do not make this a practice.

If you kept full bibliography cards when you did your research, your actual bibliography (or list of Works Cited) will be simple to produce. Alphabetize your cards and type your bibliography.

According to the *MLA Handbook,* you need all or some of the following information in a bibliography entry for a book:

1. Author's name (always);
2. Title of the part of a book (if you are referring to a part found in a collection);
3. Title of the book (always);
4. Name of the editor, translator, or compiler (if necessary);
5. Edition used (if necessary);
6. Number of volumes (if necessary);
7. Name of the series (if necessary);
8. Place of publication, name of the publisher, and date of publication (always);
9. Page numbers (for part of a book).

Begin each reference at the margin, and double space each line after the first, indenting the second and following lines five spaces from the margin. Consider the following examples:

Fielding, Henry. *Joseph Andrews*. New York: Signet, 1960.

Gibaldi, Joseph and Walter H. Achtert. *MLA Handbook for Writers of Research Papers*.
New York: The Modern Language Association of America, 1984.

Lewis, C. S. "A Play of Wit." *Twentieth Century Interpretations of* Utopia. Ed. William
Nelson. Englewood Cliffs: Prentice, 1968. 66–9.

Milton, John. *Complete Poetry and Major Prose*. Ed. Merritt Y. Hughes. New York: Odyssey. 1957.

When you provide bibliography entries for articles in periodicals, you note the following:

1. Author's name (always);
2. Title of article (in quotation marks, with a period inside the second marks);
3. Name of the periodical (underlined);
4. Series number or name (always);
5. Volume number (if necessary);
6. Date of publication (in parentheses, followed by a colon);
7. Page numbers.

Consider the following example:

Siemans, Lloyd.   "Naturalism in the Poetry of Hardy and Meredith."   *English Studies in Canada*

   3 (Spring, 1977): 51–68.

NOTE: As a general rule, use two spaces after a period and one space after all other forms of punctuation.

The key to successful documentation of sources is taking thorough and accurate notes while you conduct your research. You will find it very frustrating if you have to go back to the library, looking for a book which is no longer there, to find a page reference you neglected to note. You will make things much easier for yourself by being systematic and methodical.

EXERCISE

For questions 1 through 3, integrate the quotations in the discussions provided. If integration is not possible, append the quotations smoothly.

1. What Morag Gunn says about Gerard Manley Hopkins is true of most poets "almost always, if you can get inside the lines, you find he's saying what he means with absolute precision." (Laurence *Diviners* 183)

_____

_____

_____

_____

2. Morag works for Mr. Sampson. "Mr. Sampson is a slight, thin, rabbity little man in his mid-sixties, whose face is not strengthened by the small wavering moustache he wears. His appearance is not impressive until you notice that his greenish eyes are very clear, intelligent, and watchful." (Laurence *Diviners* 295)

_____

_____

_____

_____

3. "The Wild Swans at Coole" is a dramatic monologue;
   The nineteenth Autumn has come upon me/
   Since I first made my count;/
   I saw . . . (lines 7, 8, 9).
   Yeats uses the first person.

_____

_____

_____

_____

4. How would you present *The Diviners* in a bibliography? It was written by Margaret Laurence; published by McClelland and Stewart Limited, 25 Hollinger Road, Toronto; first printing in 1974. The edition from which you have quoted was printed and bound in Canada by T.H. Best Company, Don Mills, Ontario.

_____

_____

5. "Levels of Parody in *The Merry Wives of Windsor*" was published in *English Studies in Canada* in the Summer, 1977 edition. This was Volume III, Number 2. Ronald Huebert wrote the article, and it starts on page 129 and ends on page 135 of the journal. Provide a footnote.

_____

_____

_____

PART III

Writing about Literature

CHAPTER 7

Analysis of a Poem

Writing is a very general term. Individual types of writing assignments follow particular formats, and the work you must produce in your papers is judged both on its content and on its presentation. An essay is not an analysis; an analysis is not a research paper.

Subjecting a piece of literature to analysis is not unlike subjecting anything else to analysis. In an analysis, you consider an entity's components and see how they work together (or fail to work together). The successful merging of the appropriate components is a whole. In the case of a piece of literature, the whole is comprised of elements which act both objectively and subjectively. The complexity of this interaction, like the complexity of character traits within a single person, elicits both intellectual and emotional responses. You, as a reader of a literary piece, must consider its stimuli and the means by which they evoke responses.

You are asked to write an analysis of a piece of literature: a poem, a play, a short story, or a novel. Your assignment, then, is twofold: to *analyse* and to *write*. Before attempting your first task, analysis, you must realize something: you must consider the whole before you focus on the parts. You cannot analyse anything if you do not know it *well*. How is it possible to consider individual elements without thinking of them in the context of the whole? No element exists in a vacuum; nothing does. In the case of a poem, for example, figures of speech, images, rhyme, and metre are not independent entities; they are elements which, when put together in a particular way, comprise a particular poem.

If you try to attack a poem head-on without proper consideration, you may find yourself producing something similar to what this writer had to say:

> *The topic assigned is to analyse this poem which is a sonnet by Shakespeare who uses fourteen lines and a Shakespearean rhyme scheme which he invented to suit what he wanted to say and the pentameter line which sounded like real speech but isn't.*

Pull yourself together. Mangled presentations reflect incoherent thoughts. It is all right if your thoughts are a jumble initially, but they must be organized before they appear in your final draft. How do you order your thoughts about a poem?

KNOW THE POEM

A poem is a work of literary art. It is an entity, like a tapestry—lovely as a whole. The individual strands are woven together to make a thing of beauty. The strands may be remarkable, but they are truly effective only when woven together. A poem, too, has unifying threads, but you must see the whole piece before you unravel it. Your analysis of the poem involves unravelling the strands for the reader and then showing how they are woven together. Do not simply unravel the poem and leave the reader with a few tangled threads. Indicate why each thread (a word, an image, a rhyme, a metre) is necessary to the total effect.

It is much easier to put a jigsaw puzzle together when you have a complete picture from which to work. It is much easier to analyse a poem when you have the completed piece in your mind.

WHAT IS AN ANALYSIS?

What a poet is saying is often not so important in an analysis as *how* he or she is saying it. Thus, while every poem has a subject and some sort of "story," these things do not make the words on the poet's page a poem. Consequently, your poetry analysis is not a relation of the plot, nor a paraphrase of the poet's ideas. Plot synopsis is not your aim. Likewise, an analysis is not merely a "translation" of images to layman's terms.

Knowing the poem is comprehending the relationships of all the poetic devices that make the work a whole. How does one get to know the poem?

PENCIL IN HAND

Reading the poem, even four or five times, and *knowing* it are two different things. Since the poet is communicating with you through the written word, you must respond to him or her in kind. Explore the poem, pencil in hand. Carry on a discussion with the poet through marginal notes, underlining, and circling. This active communication with the work will provide you with the material you need to analyse the poem for your reader.

What are you looking for in the poem? Of course, rhyme and metre are important for the movement of the piece. For full appreciation of its pace and metre, read the poem aloud. While time will not always permit a careful scansion of the entire poem, particularly if the analysis is an "in class" exercise, an accomplished poetry reader will intuitively respond to rhythm and any irregularities in it. This proficiency comes with practice and should be your aim. Consider noteworthy metrical devices that vary a uniform rhythm. Note anything that is unusual or particularly effective about the metre or format of the work, but do not belabour the obvious. Regular metre should be mentioned, but not proven. Consider the effect of regular metre, but do not spend valuable time proving that it exists. Focus on exceptions and irregularities.

A discussion of metre by someone who is not capable and confident can be disastrous. The inexperienced analyst who opens a discussion of a poem with reference to the "light, skipping rhythm," or something similar, has lost credibility in the first paragraph. Avoid quicksand. Talk about something you can handle well. (See the Appendix for a discussion of metre and the vocabulary surrounding it.)

Consider the structure of the poem. Is it written in stanzas? Is the prosody of each stanza the same, similar, different? Is the poem a sonnet, an ode, a lyric? Does the subject matter dictate the structure? What is the rhyme scheme? Again, note irregularities, but do not spend time and space "reciting" a regular rhyme scheme.

Figures of speech, images, and symbols are of prime importance in a poem. These, along with prosody, are the focal points for your analysis. The implications of poetic devices and their relationships are the joining threads in the tapestry of poetry. Note devices as you read the poem aloud. Work out your own form of shorthand (for example, underline images and symbols; circle figures of speech). Once you have established that these devices exist in the work, you must consider *why* they exist.

ANALYSE THE WORK

Once you have established a familiarity with the poem to the point that you *know* it, you can explore it. You are now ready to discover the special configurations of the piece you are analysing. You know the poem when you are fully aware of what its individual components are and why they work. You must note what movement there is in the poem in terms of themes, symbols, and images. Figures of speech are the vehicles for much of this movement. Remember—these are the threads. In isolating them, you have started to unravel the poem. This unravelling should not end with merely a list of images and figures of speech. A list may help you get everything you want from the supermarket, but it will not tell you anything about a poem.

The "image listers" are an unfortunate lot in any literature course. Their essays mention the alliteration in line 1; hyperbole in line 2; personification in line 3; onomatopoeia in line 4; metaphor in line 5;. . . . The result, of course, is a badly dissected poem. It has been pulled apart haphazardly and left to die.

Certainly, in studying a poem, the individual asks what devices exist in each line. However, listing them is only one step in a complex process. How and why do the devices work? Shakespeare's devices work; Mr. X's do not. They may be the same devices. The image of the rose is not new. Some poets have used it successfully; others have not. Why? The image is an integral part of the whole in a good poem, but, in a bad poem, it is superfluous or unrelated.

Once you have unravelled the poem in terms of its devices, you must show how the poet wove the threads together. If you stop at the unravelling, you are only half done.

REWEAVE THE THREADS

The preparatory organization and the actual writing of the analysis are the next, final, and important steps in doing your analysis. You must indicate the validity of the poem in terms of whether or not its component parts work together as a whole. Here your list of symbols, devices and noteworthy prosody plays an important part.

Consider the following questions:

1. What is the dominant mood or theme? Is it consistent throughout the poem? If not, why not?
2. How does the poet create the mood and atmosphere?
3. Do the images and figures of speech work? How? Why?
4. How do the unifying threads unify?

Your responses to these questions comprise your analysis.

EXAMPLE

Consider the following poem by Archibald Lampman. Read it aloud. Notice its mood, pace, and theme. Lampman is discussing heat. Why is his discussion a poem and not a chapter of a physics textbook? Is physical heat the subject, or is it a metaphor for something other than temperature?

You should read the poem carefully at least two or three times before you try to analyse it.

"Heat"

From plains that reel to southward, dim,
The road runs by me white and bare;
Up the steep hill it seems to swim
Beyond, and melt into the glare.
Upward half-way, or it may be
Nearer the summit, slowly steals
A hay-cart, moving dustily
With idly clacking wheels.

By his cart's side the wagoner
Is slouching slowly at his ease,
Half-hidden in the windless blur
Of white dust puffing to his knees.
This wagon on the height above,
From sky to sky on either hand,
Is the sole thing that seems to move
In all the heat-held land.

Beyond me in the fields the sun
Soaks in the grass and hath his will;
I count the marguerites one by one;
Even the buttercups are still.
On the brook yonder not a breath
Disturbs the spider or the midge.
The water-bugs draw close beneath
The cool gloom of the bridge.

Where the far elm-tree shadows flood
Dark patches in the burning grass,
The cows, each with her peaceful cud,
Lie waiting for the heat to pass.
From somewhere on the slope near by
Into the pale depth of the noon
A wandering thrush slides leisurely
His thin revolving tune.

In intervals of dreams I hear
The cricket from the droughty ground;
The grasshoppers spin into mine ear
A small innumerable sound.
I lift mine eyes sometimes to gaze:
The burning sky-line blinds my sight:
The woods far off are blue with haze:
The hills are drenched in light.

And yet to me not this or that
Is always sharp or always sweet;
In the sloped shadow of my hat
I lean at rest, and drain the heat;
Nay, more, I think some blessed power
Hath brought me wandering idly here:
In the full furnace of his hour
My thoughts grow keen and clear.

In this poem, Archibald Lampman has integrated and fused a number of poetic devices to create a whole. Like all poets, he has incorporated rhyme, metre, symbols, images, and figures of speech. They work for Lampman because he successfully integrates the devices. You are to analyse his poem. To do so, you must see what devices Lampman has used and recognize the unifying elements.

Read the poem, aloud, pencil in hand. You have already read it a couple of times without touching it. Now you can carry on a marginal dialogue with the poet, and the poetic devices he has used should become apparent to you. They are more apt to do so if you read the poem aloud, because, if you do not *see* a device, you may *hear* one. In reading aloud, you cannot miss the aural devices such as onomatopoeia, alliteration, assonance, and rhyme.

Notice the stanzaic format. Are the stanzas regular? Is the rhyme scheme consistent in each stanza? Are the links between stanzas chronological, cause and effect, variations on a theme? Each stanza should prepare you for the next one, since they are the building blocks of the whole poem. Each of these stanzas is end-stopped. Is there a reason for the last line of every stanza's being trimeter, while the first seven in each block are tetrameter?

What symbols do we find in the poem? Predictably, heat is a major symbol. That is evident from the title. However, we must isolate the qualities, sources, and effects of heat as presented by the poet. Is heat related to, compared with, or contrasted with any other images or symbols? As we analyse the poem, we answer these questions.

What is the atmosphere or mood of the poem? What is its pace? How are they expressed and maintained? Do you feel the heat the speaker in the poem is describing? Why? Notice the slow pace of the poem. The words in the poem are generally monosyllabic; they plod. The rhyme is masculine, heavy, strong. Note the sustained consonants or long vowels in the rhyme sounds. There are very few light feet.

Consider the treatment of heat. Underline and make marginal notes as you analyse the poem. Note the recurring references to heat. Does the level of these references change from stanza to stanza? Is each reference within each stanza necessary? Establish the scorched, arid, dusty, quiet landscape "in the heat held-land." But is this all? Do we have to contend only with heat? Notice that the dryness is offset with wetness. Why? While the sun provides heat to the landscape, it also "drenches" it in light. The road, in the opening stanza, seems to swim—and melt. Obviously, there is a balanced tension here that the poet has carefully engineered. Continue through the poem. Your marginal notes may look like the following:

"Heat"

From plains that reel to southward, dim,   *stop — line seems long*   *4 beats*
The road runs by me white and bare;   *alliteration - r - wheel white/dry*
Up the steep hill it seems to swim   *swim - water . S's - slow, snakey*
Beyond, and melt into the glare.   *liquid - melt*
Upward half-way, or it may be
Nearer the summit, slowly steals   *fast → slow*
A hay-cart, moving dustily   *heat, dust, dry*
With idly clacking wheels.   *short line - 3 feet - summation - end-stopped*
                                            onomatopeia - circle moving
By his cart's side the wagoner   *1st character - worker*   *3 beats*
Is slouching slowly at his ease,   *alliteration - assonance - s-l-o-w*   *every stanza*
Half-hidden in the windless blur   *dust, dry, still, hot.*
Of white dust puffing to his knees.   *day - puff - onomatopeia*
This wagon on the height above,
(From sky to sky) on either hand,   *are - circle*
Is the sole thing that seems to move
In all the heat-held land.   *- assonance - abrupt stop.*

Beyond me in the fields the sun   *- speaker - 2nd character - 1st person*
Soaks in the grass and hath his will;   *Soak - liquid - hath will - Biblical - universal*
I count the marguerites one by one;   *flower - looks like wheel*
Even the buttercups are still.   *← still - stop. - followed by anapest*
On the brook yonder not a breath
Disturbs the spider or the midge.   *Quiet - nature still*
The water-bugs draw close beneath   *water - wet*
The cool gloom of the bridge.   *- spondee - assonance - abrupt stop.*

Where the far elm-tree shadows flood   *water - lots of it ←*
Dark patches in the burning grass,   *intense heat - lots of it*
The cows, each with her peaceful cud,   *Quiet*
Lie waiting for the heat to pass.   *tranquil*
From somewhere on the slope near by   *vague - haze - preparation for final line*
Into the pale depth of the noon   *vague*
A wandering thrush slides leisurely   *anapest - movement - rush in enjambment*
His thin revolving tune.

In intervals of dreams (I) hear *reality/dream, 1st person thinking, dreaming*
The cricket from the droughty ground; *assonance - slow - dry - very dry*
The grasshoppers spin into (mine) ear *anapest - fast - spin/circle - mine/Biblical*
A small innumerable sound. *indefinite, foggy (see final line)*
(I) lift (mine) eyes sometimes to gaze: *1st person - gaze/haze - foggy, dim*
The (burning) sky-line (blinds) my sight: *heat/light of sun merged*
The woods far off are blue with <u>haze</u>: *unclear*
The hills are <u>drenched in light</u>. *drench - very wet -- in light, not water*

And yet to (me) not this or that *1st person*
Is <u>always</u> (sharp) or <u>always</u> (sweet); *indefinite, not rigid/transitory) truth*
In the (sloped) (shadow) of my hat *wilting*
I lean at rest, and drain the heat; *lean - relax - regular metre*
Nay, more, I think some <u>blessed</u> power *long line - strong) arrest - Nay more ... diety*
Hath brought me wandering (idly) here: *anapest - Quick line following) show one*
In the (full) (furnace) of his hour, *assonance - spondees*   *idle wheels*
My thoughts grow keen and clear. *regular metre - equalibrium regained*
                               ultimate certainty/purifying heat.

     You see now that you have a great deal with which to work. You have expanded your dry-heat/cool-dampness dichotomy in your marginalia. What else is there to discuss? This is the point at which you isolate and arrange (perhaps in list form) the figures of speech, symbols, images, and noteworthy prosody.

1. Heat—dryness—stillness—quiet
   "hay-cart moving dustily"
   "windless blur"
   "white dust"
   "heat held land"
   "burning grass"
   "droughty ground"
   "full furnace of this hour"
   "burning skyline"—blinds (heat/light)
2. Wetness—humidity
   "road seems to swim and melt"
   "sun soaks"—"hath its will"
   "brook"
   "waterbugs"—"cool gloom"
   "shadows flood"
   "hills are drenched in light"
   "drain the heat"

     Did you notice the circle imagery? The cycle and the cyclical nature of the poem are unifying threads. They weave together the other images:

"Plains reel"
"Reel . . . road runs"
     alliteration—whirr of wheel

> "idly clacking wheels"
>   movement of poem, slow, idle
> "from sky to sky"—arc
> "bridge"—arc
> "thin revolving tune"
> "grasshoppers spin"
> "marguerites"
> "buttercups"

The circle completes and unifies.

Notice how the metrical elements are consistent with the imagery. While the prevalent foot (iambic) need not be mentioned to excess in your analysis, it does establish a regular rhythm. Metre becomes important in a poem when it results in an unexpected departure from the established rhythm, generally for a good reason. The iambic metre establishes regularity, circular repetitions consistent with the circle imagery. In addition, it establishes an equilibrium consistent with the stillness of the atmosphere. Note effective exceptions:

> Spondees (often coupled with assonance)
>   arrest motion—"cool gloom"
>   inertia—"heat-held land"
>   intensity—"full furnace"

> Anapests (often coupled with enjambement)
>   motion of quick movement
>   "wandering thrush"
>   "grasshoppers spin"
>   "into mine ear"
>   "innumerable sound"

A circular movement balances the stillness.

Who is the speaker in the poem? Do you know who the "me" of the poem is? What does he do? He is a thinker. Ultimately his "thoughts grow keen and clear." Does the heat purify his thoughts, burning off all sludge? Is this the ultimate purpose of heat?

Is there another character in the poem? What purpose does the wagoner serve? Is there perhaps another dichotomy here?—the thinker and the worker, both drenched in heat? Think about it. Can you develop this concept?

What are the predominant figures of speech? Of course, the onomatopoeia of the clacking wheels of the first stanza establishes a pace, especially since it follows the whirr of wheels in the alliterative r's of the first two lines. If the r's whirr, what do all the s's do? Don't the s's of the first stanza slow down the pace set by the r's to culminate in idle clacking rather than whirring? Continue to trace the s's. Consider assonance along with alliteration. You are collecting material for your analysis.

PULL THE PIECES TOGETHER

You know the poem. You have considered it as a whole and then unravelled it. Now put it back together. Illustrate the relaxed, slow, idle atmosphere of the poem. Discuss the heat imagery and indicate how it merges with dampness. Comment on the poet's merging of two seemingly contradictory elements. Consider the circles. How do they work? Tell your reader. Who appears in the poem? What do they signify? What poetic devices has Lampman used? How does the prosody suit the subject matter? Why does the poem work? Does it close on the same note on which it opened, or is there some change of mood or resolution of idea?

When you have answered these questions, you have rewoven the threads of the poem and written a successful poetry analysis.

PITFALLS TO AVOID

1. Your reader knows that the person who wrote the poem is a poet. It is not necessary to remind him or her of this fact. Thus while you must introduce the work and writer, your opening statement need not be, "In the poem, 'Heat,' the poet, Archibald Lampman. . . ."
2. Avoid tautologies. Do not say, "This poem is about heat." Assume your reader can read and paraphrase or summarize the content.
3. While poetry evokes both intellectual and emotional reactions, your personal, emotional reaction to the work is not suitable in a formal analysis. Focus on the emotions the poem arouses in every intelligent reader. Be as detached and objective as possible. Your past experiences on hot days are not subject matter for a formal analysis of "Heat."
4. An unravelled poem must be reassembled. Do not leave your analysis hanging. Conclude neatly and positively. Avoid "I hope you agree with me that this is a good poem." Be assertive.
5. Avoid moralizing. Do not produce for your reader a "lesson to be learned from this poem."
6. Proofread your analysis before submitting it. After all the time you have spent arranging and writing your analysis, why let a few typographical errors pull you down?

CHAPTER 8

Analysis of a Short Story

A short story is as much a work of literary art as a poem, and analysing it is not unlike analysing a poem. The poet and the short story writer use the same techniques, but with different emphases. So, too, the analyst's techniques are the same for each genre, but his or her focus changes.

In a short story, many literary devices work in conjunction to a specific end. These devices act both objectively and subjectively, evoking response from a reader. You, the reader, must analyse the short story, then, in terms of the devices and the ways in which these stimuli evoke responses; but, of course, you must first grasp the short story as a unit before considering its parts. In exploring the whole, determining the parts, and considering how the parts interrelate within the whole, you are analysing a short story.

WHAT IS AN ANALYSIS?

Before determining what an analysis *is*, you might dismiss what it is *not*. An analysis is *not* a book report. You need not write an analysis or an essay *only* to prove that you have read the work. A plot synopsis, then, is unnecessary. You should not relate "what happened to whom, where and when." Rather, you should indicate how the author, in telling "what happened to whom, where and when," has produced a work of literature and not a gossip column.

The elements of plot, character, and setting are integral to any work of fiction. You cannot avoid them in an analysis. However, a discussion of the *function* of these elements, not of their *presence,* constitutes an analysis. Knowing the story means comprehending the complex interrelationships of all the literary devices that make the work a whole.

Consider, for example, the story of an aristocratic old lady's routine existence in an old house. Perhaps you might think there would not be much to relate about Stephanie de Bichette, the old lady in question. Yet, read Anne Hébert's "The House on the Esplanade" (starting on the next page) to see how unremarkable material can be the basis of a remarkable short story. Read the story again, noting the literary elements that comprise it. You have heard or will hear about these elements in your lectures. The internal relationships among these elements differ in different stories. For the purpose of *this* discussion you are concerned only with the devices in and their impact on "The House on the Esplanade." These devices are not necessarily the same in *every* story. Adapt your analysis of a story to the elements within the fiction. Read the story, pencil in hand, considering the absence, presence, and impact of particular elements. Then consider the story in light of the discussion which follows it.

Anne Hébert (1916–   )
The House on the Esplanade
(translated by Morna Scott Stoddart)

Stephanie de Bichette was a curious little creature with frail limbs that seemed badly put together. Only her starched collarette kept her head from falling over on her shoulder; it was too heavy for her long, slender neck. If the head of Stephanie de Bichette looked so heavy, it was because all the pomp of her aristocratic ancestors was symbolized in her coiffure, a high up-swept style, with padded curls arranged in rows on her narrow cranium, an architectural achievement in symmetrical silvery blobs.

Mademoiselle de Bichette had passed, without transition period, without adolescence, from the short frocks of her childhood to this everlasting ash-grey dress, trimmed at neck and wrists with a swirl of lilac braiding. She owned two parasols with carved ivory handles— one lilac and the other ash-grey. When she went out driving in the carriage she chose her parasol according to the weather, and everyone in the little town could tell the weather by the colour of Mademoiselle de Bichette's parasol. The lilac one appeared on days of brilliant sunshine, the ash-grey one whenever it was slightly cloudy. In winter, and when it rained, Stephanie simply never went out at all.

I have spoken at length about her parasols because they were the outward and visible signs of a well-regulated life, a perfect edifice of regularity. Unchanging routine surrounded and supported this innocent old creature. The slightest crack in this extraordinary construction, the least change in this stern programme would have been enough to make Mademoiselle de Bichette seriously ill.

Fortunately, she had never had to change her maid. Geraldine served and cared for her mistress with every evidence of complete respect for tradition. The whole life of Stephanie de Bichette was a tradition, or rather a series of traditions, for apart from the tradition of the well-known parasols and the complicated coiffure, there was the ritual of getting up, of going to bed, of lace-making, of mealtimes, and so on.

Stephanie Hortense Sophie de Bichette lived facing the Esplanade, in a grey stone house dating back to the days of the French occupation. You know the sort of house *that* implies—a tall, narrow edifice with a pointed roof and several rows of high windows, where the ones at the top look no bigger than swallows' nests, a house with two or three large attics that most old maids would have delighted in. But, believe it or not, Mademoiselle de Bichette never climbed up to her attics to sentimentalize over souvenirs, to caress treasured old belongings, or to plan meticulous orgies of housecleaning amid the smell of yellowing paper and musty air that even the best-kept attics seem to possess.

No, she occupied the very heart of the house, scarcely one room on each floor. On the fourth story, only Geraldine's room remained open, among the rooms of all the former servants. It was part of the family tradition to close off rooms that were no longer used. One after another, bedroom after bedroom had been condemned: the room where the little brothers had died of scarlet fever, when Stephanie was only ten years old; the bedroom of their mother, who had passed away soon after her two children; the room of Irénée, the elder brother who had been killed in an accident, out hunting; the room of the elder sister, Desneiges, who had entered the Ursuline convent; then the bedroom of Monsieur de Bichette, the father, who had succumbed to a long illness; to say nothing of the room belonging to Charles, the only surviving brother, which had been closed ever since his marriage.

The ritual was always the same: once the occupant of the room had departed for the cemetery, the convent, or the adventure of matrimony, Geraldine would tidy everything away, carefully leaving each piece of furniture exactly in place; then she would draw the shutters, put dust-covers on the arm-chairs, and lock the door for good. No one ever set foot in that room again. One more member of the family was finally disposed of.

Geraldine took a distinct pleasure in this solemn, unvarying rite, just as a gravedigger may take pride in a neat row of graves, with well-kept mounds and smoothly raked grass above them. Sometimes she remembered that one day she would have to close Mademoiselle Stephanie's room, too, and live on for a while, the only living creature among all the dead. She looked forward to that moment, not with horror, but with pleasant anticipation, as a rest and a reward. After so many years of housework in that great house, all its rooms would be fixed at last in order, for all eternity. Mildew and dust could take possession then; Geraldine would have no more cleaning to do then. The rooms of the dead are not "done up."

This was not the calculation of a lazy woman. Geraldine dreamed of the last door closed and the last key turned in the lock just as the harvester dreams of the last sheaf of corn, or the needlewoman of the last stitch in her embroidery. It would be the crowning achievement of her long life, the goal of her destiny.

It was strange that the old servant reckoned two living people among the dead: Mademoiselle Desneiges, the nun, and Monsieur Charles, a married man and the father of a family. They had both left the family roof, that was enough for Geraldine to class them as non-existent. The heavy door of the cloister had closed forever on one, while Charles, by marrying a common little seamstress from the Lower Town, had so grieved his father that the old house and all it contained had been left to Stephanie. Charles came to see his sister every evening, but Geraldine never spoke a word to him. For her, Stephanie was the whole of the de Bichette family.

On the third floor, all the bedrooms were closed, with the exception of Mademoiselle de Bichette's. On the second, only the small blue boudoir lived on, a life of dimness and disuse. On the first floor, an immense drawing-room stretched from front to back, cluttered with furniture of different periods, each piece bristling with fussy elaborate knick-knacks. The ground-floor doors were always open, with high, carved portals to the vestibule, the parlour, the dining-room. In the basement was the old-fashioned kitchen, uncomfortable and always damp. Geraldine was the cook as well as the maid-of-all-work, but was never addressed as such.

If her mistress lived by tradition until it became a religion, Geraldine, too had her tradition, the collecting of bright-coloured buttons. Her black skirt and her white apron never changed, but she used her imagination in trimming her blouses. Red buttons sparkled on blue blouses, yellow ones on green, and so on, not to mention buttons in gold and silver and crystal. In the attic, she had discovered great chests of ancient garments which she had stripped, shamelessly, of their trimmings. Apart from this innocent craze for buttons, the big woman with the ruddy complexion made no objections to touring the wine cellar every evening before going to bed, as the last of her duties, conscientiously and even devotedly performed. But where she excelled, was in the observance of tradition where her mistress was concerned.

Every morning, at seven o'clock in summer and eight in winter, she climbed the three flights of stairs and knocked at the bedroom door. . . . Two taps, two firm, decided taps, no more, no less. This was the signal for the ceremonial to begin.

Geraldine opened the bedroom curtains, then the window curtains, and finally the shutters. Her ageing mistress preferred to sleep in complete darkness, requiring several thicknesses of material and polished wood between herself and the wicked witchcraft of the night.

She was afraid of the first rays of sunlight as well, not knowing what to do about them, since they might easily wake you long before the proper time for getting up.

Then Geraldine would return to the passage to fetch a kind of wagon equipped with everything Stephanie might need for the first few hours of the day. Two white pills in a glass of water, coffee and toast, toothbrush and toothpowder, a copper bathtub, white towels, white, starched underwear. Also a feather duster, a broom, a dustpan . . . all that she used for tidying up the room. This wagon was as wide as a single bed, four feet wide, with three shelves. Geraldine had made it herself out of old packing cases.

When Stephanie's breakfast was finished, the maid would bathe, dress, and powder her mistress, then do her hair. Stephanie allowed her to do everything, silent, inert, trusting. After that, there was sometimes a moment of painful indecision, an anguished knot in the brain of Mademoiselle de Bichette, when Geraldine leaned over to look out of the window, examining the sky and frowning as she declared:

"I really don't know what sort of weather we're going to have today."

Then the old lady would stare at her maid with such forlorn eyes that Geraldine would say, hurriedly:

"It's going to rain. You're not going to be able to go out this morning. I'll let the coachman know."

Stephanie would grow calm again after that, but she would not be entirely herself until Geraldine had settled her carefully in the blue drawing-room, on her high-backed chair of finely carved wood, near the window, her half-finished lace on her knee and her crochet hook in her hand. Only then would the idea take firm root in her brain:

"It's going to rain. I can't go out. . . . All I have to do is to handle this hook and this thread as my mother taught me to do when I was seven years old. . . . If it had been a fine day, it would have been different, I would have gone out in the carriage. There are only two realities in the world . . . only two realities I can rely on . . . and close my eyes, deep inside them: the reality of going out in the carriage, the reality of making my lace. . . . How lost and strange I am when Geraldine cannot tell what the weather is going to do, and I am left in suspense with no solid ground beneath my feet. . . . It just *wracks* my brain! Oh! Not to have to think about it, to let myself be carried away by one or the other of these my only two sure and certain realities going out for a drive or sitting here, making my lace. . . ."

Even if the day turned out fine in the end, Geraldine never said so. It would have been too much of a shock for her mistress. Imagine what confusion in such a patterned existence if someone had suddenly announced a change, after she had firmly established herself for the day in the reality of lace-making, and dared to tell her she had taken the wrong road? She could never again have believed in any reality at all.

Since her childhood, Mademoiselle de Bichette had been making lace doilies of different sizes, which Geraldine used in many different ways. These doilies flowed from her fingers at the steady rate of four per week, small pieces of white lace that resembled each other like peas in a pod. They were everywhere in the house—five or six on the piano, seven or eight on all the tables, as many as ten on every armchair, one or two on all the smaller chairs. Every knick-knack rested on a piece of delicate openwork, so that the furniture all seemed powdered with snowflakes, enlarged as if under a microscope.

In winter, and in summer, on the days when Geraldine had decided the weather was not fit for going out, Mademoiselle de Bichette would crochet all the morning, in her blue boudoir, sitting up so straight and still that she scarcely seemed real, her feet resting on a stool covered by something that was strangely like the work the old lady held in her hands.

At five minutes to twelve, Geraldine would announce:

"Mademoiselle Stephanie's luncheon is served."

At the mention of her name, the old lady would rise at once; the ritual phrase had touched a switch somewhere within her, so that without effort, without thinking, without even understanding, she would put herself slowly and ceremoniously in motion, descend the staircase and take her place at the table.

If Stephanie did go out, she invariably returned home at a quarter to twelve, so she had ample time to receive the announcement that luncheon was served with the necessary calm.

The outings of Mademoiselle de Bichette were governed by just as incredible a routine. She came out on the sidewalk with tiny steps, her frail little body bending under the weight of that enormous pile of scaffolded curls. Geraldine helped her mistress into the carriage, the coachman whipped up his horse, and the victoria started on its slow, quiet drive, invariably the same, through the streets of the little town. The horse knew the road by heart, so the coachman seized the opportunity for a short nap, his cap pulled down over his eyes, his legs stretched out, his hands folded on his stomach. He always waked up in time, as if by magic, when the drive came to an end, crying out and stretching himself, with a jolly air of surprise:

"Well, well, Mamzelle, here we are back again!"

Just as if the old fellow, when he went to sleep as the drive started, had not been quite sure he would come back when he awoke, or if his return would be to the country of the living!

Mademoiselle de Bichette would disappear into the house, on Geraldine's arm; the coachman would unharness the horse and put the carriage away; and it was all over. With regret, the townsfolk watched the disintegration of this strange conveyance, like a ghostly apparition cutting through the clear morning light . . . the ancient nag, pulling an antique carriage, with a sleepy coachman and a tiny figure like a mummy, swathed in ash-grey and lilac.

After luncheon, Geraldine would lead her mistress into the long drawing-room on the first floor, where, without ever laying her crochet aside, Stephanie would receive a few callers, and the maid would serve dandelion wine and madeleines.

The old lady never left her chair, forcing herself to hold her head high, though her neck felt as if it were breaking under the weight of her monumental coiffure. Sometimes, this constant, painful effort was betrayed by a twitch of the lips, the only change of expression that callers could ever distinguish upon that small, powdered face. Then Stephanie would ask: "How is Madame your mother?" in a voice so white and colourless that it might have come from one of the closed rooms, where, according to the gossips of the town, some of the original inhabitants still lived on.

This phrase of Stephanie's had to do for greeting, for farewell, for conversation; indeed, it had to do for everything, for the wine was sour and the madeleines stale and hard as stones. The callers were all so aged and unsteady that the most utter stranger would have had the tact never to ask that preposterous question, but Mademoiselle de Bichette knew no other formula, and in any case, she attached no importance whatever to the words she was saying. If she finished a lace doily while her callers were present, she simply let it fall at her feet, like a pebble into a pool, and began another identical piece of lace. The visiting ladies never stayed very long, and Stephanie seemed to notice their departure as little as she did their presence.

At a quarter past six, Geraldine would announce that Monsieur Charles was waiting below. The programme of the day was ticking on like the mechanism of a good Swiss watch, and the invisible wheels of Mademoiselle de Bichette responded perfectly, warning the limbs of this strange little creature that they must immediately convey her to the ground floor.

Her brother would kiss her brow and smile, rubbing his stubby-fingered hands together and remarking:

"Um-phm! It feels good in the house."

Then he would hang his overcoat up on a hall stand, while Geraldine followed his every movement with her look of triumphant disdain. With her arms crossed upon her swelling chest, she doubtless thought she looked like the statue of the Commendatore, bound on revenge. She would cast a glance of scorn on the threadbare coat, as if to say:

"Well, what did you expect? Monsieur Charles *would* get married to a chit of a girl from the Lower Town, so naturally, his father cut him off, and I locked up his room as if he were dead. If Mademoiselle Stephanie wants him here every evening, it's her own business, but *I'm* going to let him know that I'm *glad* he was thrown out, if I *am* only the servant. I know he's poor and that's his punishment for disobeying his father. He comes here because there isn't enough to eat at home. So he gobbles up our dinners and carries away on his nasty skin a bit of the warmth from our fires. . . . The good-for-nothing!"

If it were true that Charles had only one decent meal a day, it was astonishing that he was not at all thin. He was even fat, very fat, flabby and yellow-complexioned, with a bald head and a shiny face, colourless lips and almost colourless eyes. Geraldine said he had eyes like a codfish and his clothes always smelt of stale grease. Apart from that, she could not forgive a de Bichette for forgetting his table manners.

"To think that his slut of a wife has made him lose all he ever learned in decent society. . . . You wouldn't believe it possible," she would grumble to herself.

As dinner-time drew near, Charles became more and more noisily jolly. He never stopped rubbing his hands together; he got up, sat down, got up again, went from window to door and back a dozen times, while Stephanie's eyes ignored him. Then the brother and sister took their places, one at each end of the long table in the dining-room. There was no gas chandelier in this room, so it seemed even longer and darker, lit only by two tall candles in silver candlesticks. The corners of the room disappeared into the dimness, and the shadows of the brother and sister danced like black flames on the curiously carved oak panelling of the walls.

Every evening, the atmosphere of this dining-room seemed more impressive to Charles. Perhaps he felt unseen forms hiding in the darkness, invisible spectators of this singular repast; perhaps he feared to find the ghosts that haunted the bedrooms above, to see them take their places at the huge dining-table, where an old creature presided, small as a cat, white as the table-linen, who seemed already to be living in the uneasy world of phantoms.

As soon as Stephanie's brother had swallowed a few mouthfuls of soup, his good humour fell away, lifeless, utterly destroyed. When he entered the house, the smell of cooking would stimulate him, would intoxicate him with its marvellous promise, but now that the promise was kept, the man became gloomy again. Through his own bitter thoughts, he stared at the lace cloth, the heavy silverware, the fine china, and at this sister of his, who was still alive in spite of her look of belonging to some other world. What mysterious thread was keeping Stephanie here on earth? To look at her, you would have thought the slightest breath might carry her away, yet there she was, still alive.

Geraldine came and went around the table and her sharp eyes seemed to plumb the very depths of the man's thoughts. The brother sat there, knowing himself watched and understood, telling himself, in his embarrassment, that his sister would have joined her ancestors long ago had it not been for this fiendish servant, who by some diabolical process had contrived to keep the dying thing alive in her father's mansion, simply in order to enjoy as long as possible the spectacle of his own failure. In what dread "No Man's Land" of the spirit had the old witch made a pact with Monsieur de Bichette—and with Satan himself?

Geraldine had inherited all the father's anger against his son, and faithful to that anger as if to a sacred promise, she was constantly reminding Charles of the curse that lay heavy upon him. At that moment he raised his head, resenting the eyes he felt fixed upon his every movement, but Geraldine was no longer there, Charles could hear the tinkle of her keys, in the passage between the staircase and the kitchen. He shuddered, for he knew very well which keys she carried at her waist. No cupboard, no inhabited room possessed a key. It chilled his heart strangely to know that the key of his room was there, along with those of the rooms of the dead. It scared him. Then he took hold of himself again and muttered:

"This damned house! . . . Enough to drive a man crazy to sit here night after night with two cracked old fools of women. . . . The wine must have gone to my head."

But Stephanie had just got up from the table, and Charles followed her as usual.

The evening began like all the rest. Stephanie took up her lace again, while her brother walked to and fro in the long drawing-room, his hands behind his back.

And so, night after night, in complete silence, without a single word exchanged between brother and sister, the time passed until the old clock chimed ten. Then Charles, having laid up a store of warmth for the night, kissed his sister's brow, slipped on his overcoat, and with his hands in his pockets, made for Ireland Street, walking slowly along, like an idle fellow accustomed to musing as he walked.

The man followed his shadow as it flickered on the walls. The same thoughts were turning and twisting in his brain; he was used to them, as a man gets used to animals he tends every day. He knew them too well to be surprised by them; he had stopped looking at them straight in the face; they passed to and fro behind his pale eyes without ever changing his passive stare.

As he came near his own home, Charles thought of his wife. He was going back to her, in no hurry, but with a certain feeling of security, as if to a piece of property he knew belonged to him.

Suddenly, he noticed that he was nearly there. Two low houses, identical twins in misery and poverty, stood waiting for him, their tumbledown grey "stoops" jutting out to meet the sidewalk. He rented rooms on the second floor of one of these houses.

He climbed the stairs, lit a candle and went into the bedroom. A hoarse, veiled voice, a well-known voice, that could still charm him in spite of himself, said wearily:

"That you Charles?"

He set the candle on the night table. The woman shaded her eyes with her hand. He sat down on the foot of the bed.

"How's your sister?"

"Just the same."

This question, this reply, as on every other night, fell heavily into a dull silence. Beneath the words was stirring in the shadows the real meaning, unexpressed:

"Do you think your sister will last much longer?"

"Fraid so. . . . She's still hanging on. . . ."

At that moment, in the house on the Esplanade, Stephanie de Bichette was crossing her tiny cold hands on her breast and abandoning to the great empty gulf of night the small emptiness that was herself, ridiculous as an old fashion plate and dry as a pressed fig.

And Geraldine lay awake, dreaming that death had closed the last door in the old house.

PLOT

What happens in the story? How are the "events" which comprise the story presented? Does the action centre on a conflict and the resolution of that conflict? Does the action rise and fall? Are the events presented in a structural sequence?—structured chronologically?—structured some other way? Are the events dramatic?—significant?—psychological?

In Hébert's story, the events are routine and would *seem,* on first reading, to be insignificant. Read the story again. What actually happens? Does Stephanie go for a carriage ride on the day of the story or not? How do the scenes change? What is the impact of the routine visits, handiwork, and meals? Does the brother's visit differ from those of the other callers? How? How not?

CHARACTER

Who figures in a story? How is the reader introduced to the characters, and how does the reader become acquainted with them? Anybody can tell, for example, what kind of woman Stephanie de Bichette is, but how do we *get to know* her? Consider the introduction and development of characters within a literary work. Are the characters presented in an expository way? Does the narrator make direct judgments? Is the reader told what "type" the character is, or must the reader form an independent judgment? Consider the way characters are defined for the reader. Do the actions of the character define him or her? Is the presentation more dramatic than expository? Perhaps the characters are presented by analogy. Do settings, images, and symbols define the character? Do other characters act as foils? Are the characters sterotyped (a wicked step-mother, an enfeebled aristocrat, a prostitute with a heart of gold, a retainer or poor relation), or are they individual? Perhaps the characters define one another. Do the characters talk about themselves or about each other? What do they tell you?

In "The House on the Esplanade," an old woman, and her maid, driver, brother, and sister-in-law appear. Stephanie de Bichette is the *major* character the others being *minor* or secondary. How is she developed?

SETTING

Where and when does the story take place? Often the surroundings affect the plot and the characters. Think about the setting. Is it literal—a specific place and time—or is it indefinite? Is the setting atmospheric? Do items like the time of year, the weather, or the lighting depict a mood? Is a panoramic or a claustrophobic setting presented? What images are included in the setting? Are these images merely circumstantial, or do they take on meanings and, thus, become symbols? How? When?

In the short story in question no specific setting is mentioned in terms of place or time. However, there are political implications in the presentation of the aristocratic old lady whose slender neck may be supporting the old order.

The house itself is described in the same physical detail as the main character. Both are old and gray. A parallel between the house and its occupant can be drawn, and details of depiction take on symbolic meanings. Consider the similarity between Stephanie and the house and be prepared to comment on it.

POINT OF VIEW

Unlike drama or lyric poetry, novels and short stories must be narrated. Who narrates the story? The eyes and mind through which material passes affect the presentation of that material. Think about the narrator and the point of view. Is the telling of the story objective or subjective; is it biased in any way? Does an unidentified narrator tell the story, or does a character relate it? Is the narrator involved or detached? What is his or her source of information? Is the narrator's view of character external or internal?

The third-person narrator of "The House on the Esplanade" does speak in the first person at one point, and she also addresses the reader as "you" in another. However, in both instances the narrator is emphasizing the legitimacy of extended descriptions—in the first case of Stephanie's accessories, and, in the second, of Stephanie's house. The exceptions to the rule of third-person narration expose the ironic and condescending tone of the narrator: "You know the sort of house *that* implies . . . "; "but, believe it or not. . . ." The reader shares a conspiratory wink with the narrator and views Stephanie in an ironic, condescending light too.

PACE

The pace of a story reflects the rapidity with which events occur. For example, as a general rule, summary of action moves faster than dialogue. A slow pace is not bad, however, if it is appropriate; but pace is not easily accessible to criticism. Consider the pace with some caution, but do not focus on it in an analysis.

The time factor is more tangible than pace. Consider how much time is covered in the story. Is it chronological? Are there flashbacks—or fore-shadowings? Is the movement continuous from scene to scene or from time to time, or are blocks of time omitted? Do verb tenses reflect a change in pace? How much dialogue does the writer employ? Where and why? Does the narrator pause for descriptions or general reflections?

In the story in question a day is presented, but a lifetime and a whole historical and sociological epoch is evoked as well. What gives this impression? What happens in Stephanie's day? Did she go for a carriage ride or not? Does it matter? What makes one day different from another?

ANALYSIS OF THE STORY

In considering the plot, characters, setting, point of view, and pace of "The House on the Esplanade," you are gathering material for your analysis. Reread the story carefully. You might determine that the crucial structural element is the parallel between character and setting. Stephanie is the house; the house is Stephanie. Each mirrors the other. Can you prove this assertion? Do particular details corroborate your general impression? Consider *in detail* the following paragraphs taken from the opening pages of the stort story. The former, the initial paragraph of the story, introduces Stephanie; the latter, the fifth paragraph of the story, presents her house.

old? young? —physical size?

Stephanie (de) Bichette was a curious little creature with frail limbs that seemed
construction
badly put together. Only her starched collarette kept her head from falling over on her

shoulder; it was too heavy for her long, slender neck. If the head of Stephanie de Bichette
old order
looked so heavy, it was because all the pomp of her aristocratic ancestors was symbolized

in her coiffure, a high up-swept style, with padded curls arranged in rows on her narrow

cranium, an architectural achievement in symmetrical silvery blobs. . . .

politics / old order

Stephanie Hortense Sophie (de) Bichette lived facing the Esplanade, in a grey stone
ash grey
dress —lilac trim
house dating back to the days of the French occupation. You know the sort of house   *—Tone*

that implies — a tall, narrow edifice with a pointed roof and several rows of high windows,
silvery blobs
where the ones at the top look no bigger than swallows' nests, a house with two or three
Stephanie
old   *not like other old maids*
not young large attics that most old maids would have delighted in. But, believe it or not, Made- *tone*

never
named moiselle de Bichette never climbed up to her attics to sentimentalize over souvenirs, to
old
maid caress treasured old belongings, or to plan meticulous orgies of housecleaning amid the

smells of yellowing paper and musty air that even the best-kept attics seem to possess.

what she doesn't do.
what does she do?
habitual present tense routine

Both Stephanie and the house are old constructions; both represent old institutions. Their
existence more than their *activity* is stressed. Physical appearance is described, but in what terms?
Her hair is an "architectural achievement;" the house is an "edifice." While her "long, slender
neck" is topped by a row of curls, the "tall narrow edifice" sports a row of windows. Symmetry
characterizes both.

The resemblance between house and owner is striking. Continue your study of the entire story.
List relevant references. What do you find?

Stephanie *always* wears an ash-grey dress trimmed with lilac.

The house is also gray.

Stephanie's hair is described in architectural terms. She has a "monumental coiffure" of "scaffolded curls".

Her life is "a perfect *edifice* of regularity"; the routine is an "extraordinary *construction*" which, if cracked, would make her ill.

A crack in a building would result in wreckage as well.

If Stephanie's routine were altered, she would have "no solid ground beneath [her] feet".

A building must rest on *solid ground.*

Stephanie's existence is not that of a real, living person. Her life is petrified. She is like an ash-grey stone, a piece of building material. She "[sits] up so straight and still that she scarcely [seems] real".

The beat of Stephanie's heart is all that keeps the house alive. She *is* the heart and occupies "the very heart of the house".

Her heart beats; life goes on: "The programme of the day was ticking on like the mechanism of a good Swiss watch".

When her heart stops, "death [will close] the last door in the old house".

Can you find any more references? Are Stephanie and her house complementary? Does the title of the story refer only to the *house* on the esplanade? Might it also refer to the *house* of de Bichette? Take into consideration both the "house as abode" and the "house as family." Can you prove that the short story centres on the parallel between house and owner?

Extend the person/edifice parallel. Stephanie is orderly and tidy; so is her house. Consider a minor character. How is Stephanie's brother, Charles, presented? Notice that, with the entrance of Charles, verb tenses change. The habitual tenses of the first half of the story are replaced by simple tenses. Charles' entrance, then, has an impact on Stephanie and the story; he is an important secondary character. He is fat, flabby, and untidy; his house is tumbledown. Charles, then, serves as a foil for Stephanie. He returns to his wife "as if to a *piece of property* he knew belonged to him". At this point, the person as property motif is more than implied; it is articulated. Minor characters, then, are used to reinforce the concept surrounding the major character. While some people may argue, . "You are what you eat," in this story Anne Hébert seems to be saying, "You are where you live."

PREPARE YOUR ANALYSIS

Armed with proof of the relationship between the house and its owner, you can prepare to write your analysis. While *character* is the dominant literary element in the story, *setting* merges with *character*. Stagnation and arrest in *character* and *setting* result in a slow-moving *plot*.

Refer to your list of references. Will you use all or some of them in your analysis? Arrange the points in order of importance. Be prepared to analyse, explain, or expand these points. Remember—you refer to the text not to *retell* the story. You are *analysing,* not *reporting.* References to the text support your analysis. Use the text as a reference point, not as a source of padding your own work.

Now you are ready to write.

WRITING THE ANALYSIS

Introduce the author and story. Indicate the structure of the work, focusing in this case on the person/edifice complement. A comment on the structure is not a thesis. It is a crucial literary statement indicating the composition of the short story under discussion.

Explore the remarkable similarity between the woman and the house, adding the further similarity between her brother and his home. Show how physical appearances correspond. Note the absence of emotional and intellectual aspects of the characters. Indicate how, in this case, *character* and *setting* dictate a minimal *plot. AVOID PLOT SYNOPSIS.*

ANALYSE ANOTHER STORY

Select a different short story. Read, reread, and analyse. How does it compare with "The House on the Esplanade"? If you can answer this question, you can feel comfortable when you write an analysis as a class assignment.

PART IV

Elements of Grammar

CHAPTER 9

Sentence Structure

Your analyses and essays are comprised of paragraphs. The composition of the paragraph is a series of sentences. What comprises these sentences? Yes, words, but how many words and in what order?

WHICH WORDS WHERE?

A sentence is more than just random *words*. Our language is ordered by grammatical rules which provide formulae for putting the appropriate words together to make sentences. While generally these rules are logical, they are frequently overlooked by the writer who becomes too involved in the *content* of what he or she is writing to consider the *presentation*. In order for your *content* to be clear, your *manner* must be logical and acceptable. You are not engaging in creative writing in your English literature assignments. Rather, you are writing expository prose. Thus, you have no poetic licence and you are not free to investigate new levels of expression. You must apply established grammatical rules and write clearly and logically.

Often incorrect grammar confuses or even negates what a writer means to say. Unravelling a garbled presentation is no fun for any reader at any time. Your essays are not necessarily the most exciting reading in the world; they would never make the best sellers list. However, they should be grammatically clear and structurally sound.

You do not make points very strongly when there is no agreement within sentences or when modifiers are attached to the wrong words. When your presentation is not clear, you give the impression that what you have to say may not be worth the trouble of deciphering it. If not presented clearly, your content cannot be considered at its true worth. If eliciting your material requires mental contortions on the part of the reader, he or she may not think your material is worth the trouble. As a result, you may lose your reader's attention and your arguments will be lost.

HOW MUCH GRAMMAR DO I HAVE TO KNOW?

Writing grammatically correct and structurally sound sentences does not require a very sophisticated familiarity with dozens of rules and exceptions to them. Often, grammar is just a question of logic. For example, you do not have to remember the term "antecedent" to recognize that a pronoun must replace a particular noun. In addition, you may never have to distinguish

87

between a present participle and a gerund so long as you *use* them correctly.

The following discussions of grammatical points present rules. You should focus on the logic inherent in the English language rather than on terms. Obsession with memorizing rules and terms can prevent real assimilation of the principles. Once you are familiar with the principles, you can label the terms. If the logic of the principles is clear, you will perhaps assimilate the rules to the point at which you can articulate them. However, *applying* the rules is crucial; *reciting* them is not. In fact, you could probably get through life never having learned what "broad pronoun reference" is. That is acceptable, so long as your pronouns do not, in fact, refer broadly. It is, of course, helpful to be familiar with grammatical terminology, but correct *use,* not *theory,* of grammatical points is your goal.

PROBLEM AREAS

The problem areas which will be discussed in this chapter are often troublesome to writers. However, these problems are not insurmountable and can be corrected easily. In fact, you could get to the point at which you avoid the errors altogether and do not have to correct them at all.

We will start at the beginning with subject and verb agreement, then move on to pronoun agreement and reference, continue with modifiers, and finish with balanced, parallel constructions. If you master these points, you will be able to write more clearly and correctly. That is not a bad position to be in.

SUBJECT AND VERB AGREEMENT

You know that every sentence you write has a minimum of a subject (noun or pronoun) and a predicate (verb). Generally, sentences contain more than these two elements, particularly sentences in formal exposition. However, the subject and the verb are the skeleton of the sentence; they support additional words. You, as a writer, must be conscious of your subjects and verbs, making them evident to a reader. The agreement between subject and verb is crucial.

A verb agrees with its subject in person and number. Often, we do not stop to consider person and number when producing a verb for a particular subject. Familiarity and comfort with the English language breed a "gut" instinct with regard to which form of a verb to use. However, sometimes the principle of agreement must be consciously applied.

"Person" indicates whether the subject is first, the speaker (I, we); second, the person spoken to (you); or third, the person or thing spoken about (he, she, it, they). "Number" indicates whether the subject is singular or plural. Generally, the third person is used in expository writing. Consequently, the issue is generally a question of whether the verb should be singular or plural (He *writes,* whereas they *write*).

Consider the following rules. The subjects in the examples are underlined.

I. If the subject of the verb is singular, the verb will be singular; if the subject is plural, the verb will be plural. This is the case regardless of what *noun* immediately precedes the verb. The *subject* always dictates whether the verb is singular or plural.

The student was late for class every day.

The subject student is singular; the verb was is singular.

The professor for each of my courses is very qualified.

The subject is professor and is singular. The fact that a plural noun courses immediately precedes the verb has no bearing on the number of the verb.

The assignments were very difficult.

The subject assignments is plural; the verb were is plural.

The assignments for the physics course are very heavy.

The subject is assignments and is plural. The fact that a singular noun course immediately precedes the verb has no bearing on the number of the verb.

II. A collective noun is used to indicate a group of people, or a group of things, like a club, a team, a deck (of cards). Generally this group is considered a unit. If this is the case, the noun and verb are singular. If, however, the *members* or *units* within the collective noun are the subject, then the subject is considered to be plural, as is the verb.

The class meets at 9:30 in room 86.

There are perhaps thirty people in the class. However, when they meet in the classroom, those thirty people are a unit, listening to one lecture, which is given once to all the class. The class, in this case, is singular.

The class are writing their essays this week.

There are still perhaps thirty people in the class. However, these individuals are not writing essays in unison. At thirty different places and at thirty different times students for the one particular class are writing essays. Thus, in this instance, class is plural and the verb is plural.

III. If subjects are joined by "and," they are considered to be plural and they take a plural verb, *unless* both subjects comprise a single unit.

Rhyme and metre are important elements of a poem.

Rhyme and metre can be replaced with they. The subject is plural; the verb should be plural.

My friend and colleague is having a party.

Joe Smith is both my friend and my colleague. My friend and colleague can be replaced with he. The subject is one person and is therefore singular. Consequently, the verb is singular.

And is the only conjunction which can join subjects, making them plural. Anything that means and, but is phrased differently, does not pluralize a subject. Phrases such as along with, as well as, in addition to, accompanied by, with, and so on, do not have the same grammatical function as and.

Donne, Traherne, and Crashawe are metaphysical poets.

BUT

Donne, as well as Traherne and Crashawe, is a metaphysical poet.

Donne is the subject. The as well as phrase does not pluralize it.

IV. If subjects are joined by *or* or *nor*, the verb agrees with the subject closest to it. If the closest noun is singular, the verb is singular; if the closest noun is plural, the verb is plural.

Either the neighbours or the <u>caretaker</u> complains about the noise every weekend.

BUT

Either the caretaker or the <u>neighbours</u> complain about the noise every weekend.

Neither the professor nor the <u>tutorial leaders</u> were happy with the exam results.

BUT

Neither the tutorial leaders nor the <u>professor</u> was happy with the exam results.

V. The subject need not necessarily come *before* the verb in order to dictate whether the verb is singular or plural. It is easy to make a mistake in agreement if the subject follows the verb. However, the verb must agree with the subject regardless of where the subject occurs in the sentence.

When were the library <u>books</u> returned?

<u>Books</u> is the plural subject. It follows the auxiliary verb since this is an interrogative sentence. However, <u>books</u> is still the subject, and the verb <u>always</u> agrees with the subject.

There is no <u>reason</u> why you should write incorrectly.

<u>Reason</u> is the singular subject indicating that the verb <u>is</u> must be singular.

VI. The following subjects are *always* singular and consequently, *always* require a singular verb: EACH, EVERY, EITHER, NEITHER, ANYONE, ANYBODY, SOMEONE, SOMEBODY, EVERYONE, EVERYBODY, NO ONE, NOBODY.

<u>Every member</u> of the tutorial <u>expects</u> to finish his or her essay on time.

BUT

<u>All the members</u> of the class <u>expect</u> to pass the exam.

<u>Neither</u> of us <u>expects</u> to find a job.

BUT

<u>We do not expect</u> to make much money.

Since <u>no one objects</u>, the meeting is closed.

BUT

<u>No members object</u>, so the meeting is closed.

It is easy to forget this principle. If you are one of the many people who are not familiar with it, give it some thought and focus on the logic of the grammar involved.

VII. If the subject of the sentence is PART OF, SOME OF, NONE OF, or MOST OF a noun or pronoun, the last noun or pronoun completing the _____ of phrase dictates whether the verb is singular or plural.

NOTE: *PARTS OF anything are plural.*

Part of the <u>lesson</u> was difficult.

Part of the <u>assignments</u> were difficult.

<u>Parts</u> of the lesson were difficult.

Some of the <u>students</u> are getting good marks.

None of the <u>game</u> was very exciting.

Most of the <u>writers</u> on the course are novelists.

This rule is very similar to the "or" or "nor" rule (IV). Think about them together: they both subscribe to the same principle.

VIII. Relative pronouns (who, which, and that) refer to a noun or pronoun. This noun or pronoun which they follow is the antecedent. Relative pronouns can refer to singular or plural antecedents (the man, who; the men, who). The antecedent determines whether the relative pronoun is singular or plural and, in turn, whether the verb in the relative clause is singular or plural.

He is one of those <u>teachers who care</u> about their students.

<u>Teachers</u> is plural; <u>care</u> is plural.

He is a <u>teacher who cares</u> about his students.

<u>Teacher</u> is singular; <u>cares</u> is singular.

I am reading a <u>book which is</u> very interesting.

<u>Book</u> is singular; <u>is</u> is singular.

I like <u>books which are</u> about travel.

<u>Books</u> is plural; <u>are</u> is plural.

EXERCISE 1

In the following sentences, you are given a choice between a singular and a plural verb. Decide which noun dictates the person and number of the verb. Each sentence is covered by one of the preceding rules. If you are not certain about a particular sentence, find the appropriate rule and apply it.

1. The professor as well as the students (thinks, think) the room is too small.
2. We are studying Hume. The man and thinker (is, are) a great philosopher.
3. She is one of those students who (is, are) never satisfied with their marks.
4. The football team (hopes, hope) to win the championship.
5. Neither the dean nor the professors (likes, like) the new ruling.
6. Both the movie and the book (relies, rely) heavily on primary sources.
7. The tensions of university life (has, have) been troubling him.
8. The Group of Seven (is, are) having a showing in the gallery.
9. Neither of us (expects, expect) to attend the general meeting.
10. The club welcomes anyone who (subscribes subscribe) to its philosophies.
11. The class (is, are) writing a very difficult exam which (counts, count) for 30% of the grade.
12. Only one of the five drivers in the races (has, have) competed before.
13. Most of the students (prefers, prefer) take-home exams.
14. Everyone who works during the year (is, are) obliged to fill out an income tax return.
15. He is one of those people who always (succeeds, succeed).
16. Although not everyone who was invited came, the celebrations (seem, seems) to have been a great success.
17. Either the television or the movies (keeps, keep) me entertained.
18. Not everyone, though many citizens would not believe it, (votes, vote) in the elections.
19. Rock and Roll (was, were) a popular music, but Rhythm and Blues (is, are) more popular now. Country and Western (is, are) popular too.
20. When (have, has) the faculty submitted the grades?
21. There are channels through which an appeal (is, are) made.
22. The student, along with her roommate, (oversleeps, oversleep) every morning.
23. Figures of speech and style (is, are) considered in a poetry analysis.
24. It is I who (am, is, are) to present the seminar tomorrow.
25. Some of his sentences (is, are) difficult to understand.

EXERCISE 2

Put the information in each of the following selections into one sentence. Take care that your subjects and verbs agree with one another.

1. I am writing an analysis of a short story.
   Plot, setting, and character are important considerations.
   Setting is the most noteworthy.

   _____

   _____

2. The Romantics are nineteenth century poets.
   The Victorians are nineteenth century poets.

   _____

   _____

3. There is a meeting of the committee tomorrow.
   Some members arrived today.
   Others will arrive tomorrow.

   _____

   _____

4. Helen, Carole, Susan, and Jean are taking that course.
   They all expect to pass.

   _____

   _____

5. I have never gotten a parking ticket.
   Andrew hasn't gotten one either.

   _____

   _____

6. The students assembled at the computer terminal.
   The system was "down."
   The class was cancelled.

   _____

   _____

7. The library was closed all day on Christmas.
   The post office was closed too.

   _____

   _____

8. He is not a unique politician.
   He promises more than he delivers.

   _____

   _____

9. The workers demanded an increase in wages.
   They want better benefits as well.
   The union supports them.

   _____

   _____

10. Will students of the 1980's resemble students of the 1970's?
    Will grades be important to them?
    Will they have original ideas?

    _____

    _____

PRONOUN AGREEMENT AND REFERENCE

Pronouns are one of the most troublesome parts of speech in English grammar. This situation is a strange situation since the rules for pronouns and pronoun agreement are the most logical of grammatical rules. A pronoun is *pro*—for—a noun. It replaces, refers back to, a particular noun. Since the *pro*noun stands *for* a noun, the writer must provide a noun for the pronoun to be *for*. The basic rule is as simple as that.

Problems with pronouns often arise because the writer is not aware that he or she and the reader are not necessarily on the same wavelength. It is patently clear to the writer who "he" is in the sentence in question. However, since the reader has not followed the same thought processes as the writer, he or she is often confused—and with good reason. If your reader cannot make out whom or what you are discussing, he or she cannot very well assimilate the content of your essay or analysis. Your ideas are not clear and you leave the reader in a state of frustration; you are both unhappy. If you apply the following rules, you will make your writing clearer to read and put your reader in a better frame of mind when he or she assesses your arguments. Using pronouns correctly is worth the effort.

This section deals with the three basic pronoun agreement rules and the four problem areas of faulty pronoun reference. Think about the inherent logic and apply the principles to your own writing.

<u>NOTE</u>: The least effective way of correcting pronoun reference and agreement problems is by eliminating pronouns. People who have tried this have not been successful. Avoiding pronouns is unnatural. Do these sentences sound natural?

The class likes the class's professor.

John submitted John's assignment.

Pronouns are necessary. Use them, but use them correctly.

PRONOUN AGREEMENT

I. A pronoun agrees with its antecedent (the word it is *pro* or for; the word to which it refers; the word it replaces) in person and number and gender. Person indicates the narrative position of the pronoun (first person, the speaker—I, me, we, us; second person, spoken to—you, yours; third person, spoken about—he, she, it, they, him, her, them). Number indicates whether the pronoun is singular (he, she, it), or plural (they). Gender is masculine, feminine, or neuter.

When Milton woke his daughter, he told her to take dictation.

In this sentence *his* and *he* refer to Milton; they are third person, singular, masculine. *Her* refers to daughter; it is third person, singular, feminine. The reader knows who *his, he,* and *her* replace because the nouns to which the *pro*nouns refer are mentioned; their proximity to the pronouns makes them obvious antecedents.

II. A collective noun is used to indicate a group of people, or a group of things, like a club, a team, a herd (of elephants). Generally the group is considered a unit. If this is the case, the noun is considered to be singular and is referred to by a singular pronoun. If, however, the *members or units* within the collective noun are being considered, the noun is considered to be plural and the pronoun referring to it is plural. (See Section II of Subject and Verb Agreement.)

The committee held its meeting at 10:00.

The committee may be composed of five, ten, or twenty members. However, these members are meeting as a unit, around *one* table in *one* room at a particular time. Thus, the committee is singular and is replaced by *its*.

The class were assigned to their tutorial groups.

There are perhaps ninety people in the class. However, there are six tutorial groups of fifteen each. At six different places and at six different times these groups meet. As a result, the class is comprised of six groups and the *class* as *groups* is replaced by the plural pronoun, *their*.

III. The following antecedents are *always* singular and, consequently, are *always* replaced by a singular pronoun: EACH, EITHER, NEITHER, ANYONE, ANYBODY, EVERYONE, EVERYBODY, SOMEONE, SOMEBODY, NO ONE, NOBODY.

NOTE: This rule is often misapplied. Perhaps the reason is the fact that the plural pronoun *they* is asexual and not offensive. However, *grammatically* the singular pronoun, he, can refer to either sex. If one finds this use offensive, he or she can write "he or she."

Has every student submitted his essay?
Has every student submitted her essay? (in a class of female students)
Has every student submitted his or her essay?

NOTE: *Every* is singular and must be replaced by a *singular* pronoun. Thus, "Has every student submitted their essay?" is incorrect.

It is possible to retain the plural pronoun if the antecedent is changed to a plural noun.
Have *all the students* submitted *their* essays?

FAULTY PRONOUN REFERENCE

I. Ambiguous or Unclear Reference

Often when you write you use more than one noun prior to a pronoun in a sentence. *You* know which noun is the antecedent because your chain of thought is clear to *you*. However, the reader may not know to which word the pronoun refers. If this is the case, the reader may be confused and may even misread the sentence. You must construct your sentence in such a way that it is clear to the reader which *noun* is the antecedent.

Writers like Swift and Defoe wrote about travellers and adventures, and they compared life to a journey.

Who or what are *they* in this sentence? Are they *writers, Swift and Defoe, travellers,* or *adventures*? The antecedent could be any one of the four. The reader has one chance in four of reading this sentence correctly. Would you want to risk your argument on these odds? A reader cannot assess what this writer is saying because he or she is not sure what the writer is implying. Rewrite the sentence.

Writers like Swift and Defoe, who wrote about travellers and adventures, compare life to a journey.

In this instance, the antecedent is clear. Did you read *Swift and Defoe* as the antecedent in the first version of the sentence? If you were the reader, which sentence would you prefer to find in an essay?

II. Misplaced Relative Pronoun Reference

The relative pronouns (who, which and that), like all pronouns, must have antecedents. The rule of thumb for relative pronoun reference is that the pronoun refers to the noun closest to it. Thus, *who, which,* or *that* should be placed as near as possible to its antecedent.

Arnold wrote an essay for his English courses <u>which</u> required a lot of revision.

In this sentence, the quality of Arnold's essay is not an issue. It would seem, however, that his English course is not in very good shape (the *course* which required a lot of revision). Presumably, this is not what the writer meant to say.

For his English courses, Arnold wrote an essay <u>which</u> required a lot of revision.

In this sentence no mention is made of the quality of the English course. Rather, it is Arnold's *essay* which required a lot of revision.

Notice that both the preceding sentences are identical in their make-up. The word order is the only difference between the two sentences. Could it be said that the whole is equal to the sum of its parts?

A writer may easily and frequently slip into the error of misplaced relative pronoun reference. The reason for this is that he or she is not organized. That is to say, when the writer begins to write a sentence, he or she does not know how, where, or when that sentence will end. After writing, for example, "Arnold wrote an essary for his English course," the writer paces the floor, sips some coffee, or makes a phone call, then returns to the piece of writing and decides to comment on the quality of Arnold's essay. However, the writer inadvertently comments on the quality of the closest noun—the English course.

Think before you write, and think again when you have written and are rereading.

III. Broad Relative Pronoun Reference

The pronouns *which, this,* and *that* are perhaps the most widely and incorrectly used pronouns in student essay writing. *Which, this,* and *that* are pronouns. That is all they are. They are not strong words. A pronoun can replace a noun; it cannot replace a phrase, an idea, a clause, a sentence, or a paragraph. It is not strong enough. It replaces a particular noun, not a *broad* idea.

Leonard Cohen is a beautiful loser <u>which</u> is why his novel is so real.

What is *which* doing in this sentence? It is meant to refer to *Cohen's being a beautiful loser,* but this is grammatically impossible. The most *which* can replace is *loser,* and *loser* is not enough.

It is difficult to correct sentences with broad pronoun reference errors without juggling the entire sentence. Reverse the opening and closing material:

(1) Leonard Cohen is a beautiful loser
(2) Which is why his novel is so real.

Reverse (1) and (2):

(1) Leonard Cohen's novel is very real
(2) Since he, himself, is a beautiful loser.

Reverse the following sentence:

It's cloudy out, which means it might rain.
It might rain because it's cloudy out.

Watch *which, this,* and *that.* Be sure they modify particular nouns. If they do not, get rid of them and rewrite the sentence.

IV. Weak or Implied Pronoun Reference

In order for a *pro*noun to be *for* a noun, to replace a noun, the noun must exist in black and white. A pronoun cannot replace a noun which does not exist, even if it is implied. Remember—a pronoun is a relatively weak and dependent piece of speech. It cannot exist on its own. Give it the support of a noun.

I found the lemonade refreshing because it was so hot and humid.

What is *it* in this sentence? Grammatically the writer has said that the lemonade was hot and humid. This is hardly refreshing. Granted, the weather is *implied,* but, unfortunately, implication is not enough.

If a pronoun does not replace a noun, the pronoun is not fulfilling its function. Supply an antecedent for the pronoun.

I found the lemonade refreshing because the day was so hot and humid.

In this sentence the day, and not the lemonade, is hot and humid. This sentence is grammatically correct.

The rules for pronoun agreement and reference are very logical. A pronoun refers to a noun; the writer must provide the noun and place it as closely as possible to the pronoun. If there are several nouns in the sentence, recast the sentence to avoid confusion. This logic allows no room for errors in pronoun agreement and reference.

EXERCISE 1

In each of the following sentences, pronouns are misused. They are lacking in either agreement or appropriate reference. Often correcting the sentence will involve rewriting it. If this is necessary, do so. In some cases, however, you need only replace a pronoun with the appropriate noun.

1. Harry has been on a diet and has lost thirty pounds which certainly improves his figure.

   _____

   _____

2. Every reader has their individual interpretation of a poem.

   _____

   _____

3. When Sylvia visited her friend in Winnipeg, she took her out to dinner.

   _____

   _____

4. Milton presents Adam and Satan in *Paradise Lost* and makes him the personification of evil.

   _____

   _____

5. One should be careful of their grammar when writing essays.

   _____

   _____

6. The car barely made it to the garage which was broken down.

   _____

   _____

7. Everyone crowded into the auditorium so that they could hear the featured speaker.

   _____

   _____

8. The poems in this collection are a good choice because it gives a good cross section of styles.

   _____

   _____

9. Bertrand got an A on his essay which made him very happy.

_____

_____

10. As soon as Betty heard that her sister had had a baby girl, she rushed to see her.

_____

_____

11. John Locke is a great philosopher which I have always admired.

_____

_____

12. Although she has never done it professionally, Mrs. Evans loves to sing.

_____

_____

13. She read her paper to the seminar which was very good.

_____

_____

14. Audiences take a while to get settled when you first go into the theatre.

_____

_____

15. These lessons are very worthwhile because it gives the students an understanding of the material.

_____

_____

16. He is very proud of his antelope antlers because they are very hard to catch.

_____

_____

17. Every member of the team will try their best in the championship game.

_____

_____

18. I couldn't find the book on the library shelf which really annoyed me.

_____

_____

19. The class will write their final exam on April 24.

_____

_____

20. I went home early because it was boring at the party.

_____

_____

21. When Gertrude heard that the nurse had in her possession the results of her blood test, she phoned her.

_____

_____

22. Every professor submitted their own grades.

_____

_____

23. The committee submitted their recommendation which was a load off everyone's mind.

_____

_____

24. She doesn't wear old jeans anymore which makes her seem more professional.

_____

_____

25. The speakers were interrupted by hecklers; some of them were very outraged.

_____

_____

EXERCISE 2

Put the information in each of the following sections into one coherent sentence. Pay special attention to pronoun reference.

1. When they visited Toronto, the family went to the Royal Ontario Museum.
   They also went to the Science Centre.
   The younger children preferred the Science Centre.

   _____

   _____

2. Paul went to the library to do some research for his essay.
   Each book he needed was in circulation.
   Paul was frustrated.

   _____

   _____

3. Helen wanted to go out to dinner.
   Jane wanted to go to a film.
   They stayed home, watched television, and sent out for a pizza.

   _____

   _____

4. The computer course deals with theory.
   The computer course allows for practice.
   Some students prefer theory.
   Some students prefer practice.

   _____

   _____

5. The car was making strange noises on the 401.
   It broke down as soon as we pulled into the driveway at home.
   We were relieved that we didn't break down on the highway.

   _____

   _____

DANGLING AND MISPLACED MODIFIERS

A modifier defines or describes another word. The rule is clear enough. An adjective modifies a noun; an adverb modifies a verb, an adjective, or another adverb. These rules are basic. Generally writers do not have trouble with straightforward adjectives or adverbs. However, *adjectival* and *adverbial* constructions do not always seem so cut and dried as *adjectives* and *adverbs*. A group of words defining or describing a noun is adjectival, and likewise, a group of words modifying a verb, adjective, or adverb is adverbial.

ADJECTIVAL CONSTRUCTIONS

The point to remember about these constructions is that they modify *nouns*. The noun must exist in order to be modified. If the sentence does not indicate which *noun* is being defined or described, the modifier "dangles"; it just hangs there, and, if it were to be attached to an existing noun, this noun would be the wrong one. If the construction, in fact, modifies the wrong noun, it is said to be "misplaced." Correcting such errors is merely a matter of common sense. First, decide which word is being modified and then place the adjectival construction as closely as possible to it.

VERBALS

There are some constructions that, at first sight, do not appear to be adjectival constructions. In fact, they do not look like adjectives at all, but rather like verbs. These words find their roots in verbs, but are used to modify nouns; they are verbals: participles, gerunds, and infinitives. Notice the verb "to swim" in the following sentences:

Swimming is good exercise.

Swimming (a gerund) is used as the subject of the sentence; it is used as a noun.

After swimming in the pool, I feel refreshed.

Swimming (a gerund) is used as a noun; it is the object of the preposition *after*. *Swimming* modifies the agent *I*.

I saw my professor swimming in the pool.

Swimming (a present participle) is used adjectivally to modify *professor*, the agent.

To swim in the university pool, you must have an activities card.

To swim (an infinitive) is used adjectivally in reference to the agent, *you*.

Notice that each of these verbals requires an *agent*. A verbal, like a verb, is an action word. Someone, or something, must perform the action implied in the verbal. This someone or something is an *agent*, the word modified by the adjectival construction containing a verbal.

PRESENT PARTICIPLE

Generally, the present participle follows immediately the *agent* (noun or pronoun) that it defines or describes (the man, *swimming* . . .). However, if a writer varies his or her sentence construction, he or she sometimes opens a sentence with a participle. If you do so (and it is fine to vary sentence structure this way), you must be sure to indicate the *agent* later in the same sentence. (*Swimming* in the pool . . .). In addition, the agent must be placed as near as possible to the participle, since the participle modifies the closest agent.

Swimming in the pool, I saw my professor.

   I am swimming.

Swimming in the pool, my professor waved to me.

   My *professor* is swimming.

Consider the following sentence:

Calling the meeting to order, a fly buzzed around the speaker's head.

   Who (or what) is calling? Yes, the fly. This is what the sentence says grammatically. However, this is probably not what this writer meant to say.

   In order to correct this sentence, the writer must attach the voice calling the meeting to order to the speaker, and not to the fly. Sometimes the best way to do so is to eliminate the adjectival participle.

Calling the meeting to order, the speaker waved a fly from his face.

   This sentence changes the emphasis of the earlier one. The irritating buzz of the fly is gone.

A fly buzzed around the speaker's head as he was calling the meeting to order.

   Here the speaker is speaking and the fly is buzzing. The sentence is clear.

GERUND

Like the present participle, the gerund (verbal noun), when used in an adjectival construction, must be attached to an agent. The person or thing performing the action implicit in the gerund must be there in black and white as near as possible to the gerund. As is the case with participial openers, a sentence beginning with a prepositional phrase containing a gerund may provide variety in sentence structure. However, you must be careful to include the agent in the sentence.

After reading Moll Flanders, Moll moves from innocence to experience.

   Who has read *Moll Flanders*? This writer indicates that Moll, herself, has read the book. Clearly this isn't what the writer meant to say.

After reading Moll Flanders, the reader sees that Moll moves from innocence to experience.

   Here the reader is reading. In spite of its redundancy (reading, reader), the sentence is clearer than the first.

In Moll Flanders, the heroine clearly moves from innocence to experience.

This sentence is clear and, at the same time, is not redundant.

INFINITIVE

When an infinitive phrase begins a sentence, care must be taken that the infinitive has an agent in the sentence. Remember—an infinitive is a verbal and, as such, implies action. Someone or something must perform this action, and this someone or something must exist in the sentence.

To get to my house, the Dundas bus is taken.

Who is getting to my house? As far as one can tell from this sentence, the *bus* is getting there. However, the *bus* is not meant to be the agent in this sentence.

To get to my house, you take the Dundas bus.

A passenger has now been provided for the bus and an agent is getting to my house. This sentence is clear and correct.

A good rule of thumb for this particular infinitive construction is that *the principal clause must be in the active, rather than the passive, voice.* Active voice provides an agent, whereas passive voice does not.

SPLIT INFINITIVES

The infinitive is comprised of two words: *to* and a verb. The English language is unique in this. In other languages the infinitive is only one word. Writers of English should consider the infinitive as *one word* (e.g., *to be*) and try never *to split* or separate the infinitive.

I tried to clearly and succinctly give my seminar.

This writer has split *to* and *give.*

I tried to give my seminar clearly and succinctly.

GENERAL RULE FOR ALL ADJECTIVAL CONSTRUCTIONS

A modifier should be placed as near as possible to the noun it is modifying.

ADVERBIAL CONSTRUCTIONS

It is easy to "misplace" an adverbial modifier. This is particularly true when the issue foremost in a writer's mind is *content* rather than *grammar.* Decide what word a modifier defines or describes; then, place the modifier as closely as possible to it.

They sang while I danced very loudly.

In this sentence, foot stomping appears to drown out the song. Place the element of noise in the appropriate place.

They sang <u>very loudly</u> while I danced.

LIMITING ADVERBS

While an adverb generally modifies a verb, modifying verbs is not its only function. Consider the following sentences:

I read <u>quickly</u>.

Quickly is an adverb, modifying the verb, *read.*

I read <u>very</u> quickly.

Very is an adverb, modifying the adverb, *quickly.*

My eyes are <u>quite</u> tired after a lot of reading.

Quite is an adverb, modifying the adjective, *tired.*

An adverb can modify a verb, adverb, or an adjective. Limiting *adverbs* (such as hardly, barely, almost, just, about, merely, only) seldom modify *verbs.* However, writers often place them next to verbs. Consider the following examples:

To get to the park from the university, you <u>only</u> drive three miles.

This writer has, in fact, just said that the only means of transportation between the park and the university is automobile. You only *drive*; you can't walk, jog, roller skate, hitchhike, or take a bus; you *only drive.* The distance is immaterial; the mode of transportation is accentuated.

To get to the park from the university, you drive <u>only</u> three miles.

Here, the distance between the university and the park is the issue, rather than the means of covering this distance.

Watch your limiting adverbs. It is much too easy to misuse them.
In fact, watch all your modifiers. Be sure that your grammar does not distort your meaning.

EXERCISE 1

Each of the following sentences contains a misplaced or dangling modifier. Correct each one by rewriting the sentence clearly and concisely. Remember—decide what word a modifier describes; then, reconstruct the sentence, placing the modifier as near as possible to the word it modifies.

1. I looked for a piano for my grandfather with a mahogany finish.

_____

_____

2. After reading *Paradise Lost,* Milton is a great poet.

_____

_____

3. Robertson Davies was able to imaginatively use the narrative technique.

_____

_____

4. To pass the course, both course work and the final exam must be passed.

_____

_____

5. The dog tried to run away from his master on a leash.

_____

_____

6. When light and fluffy, you put the meringue on the pie.

_____

_____

7. Listening to the French tapes in the language lab, Joe's pronunciation improved.

_____

_____

8. The professor tries to always make his lectures interesting.

_____

_____

9. He almost lived to be a hundred.

_____

_____

10. After jogging every morning, a glass of iced tea is very refreshing.

_____

_____

11. Vincent has a drinking problem; he nearly drinks a case of beer almost every day.

_____

_____

12. Walking down the street, the girl on the bicycle nearly knocked me over.

_____

_____

13. Reading *Huckleberry Finn,* Mark Twain presents some complex characters.

_____

_____

14. Before being fertilized, we weeded the garden.

_____

_____

15. George almost drove eighty miles an hour on the way home from Toronto.

_____

_____

16. Checking the shelf, the library book was in the wrong place.

_____

_____

17. I was very upset when, after rushing to class, my professor had cancelled it.

_____

_____

18. I only hope I get a C in this course.

_____

_____

19. After studying the Middle Ages, their customs are very interesting.

_____

_____

20. To understand the literature, the culture must be studied.

_____

_____

21. Analyzing his poetry, Donne must be a metaphysical poet.

_____

_____

22. To get seats for the play, reservations must be made in advance.

_____

_____

23. I hoped he wouldn't ask me about the book; I only read half of it.

_____

_____

24. Looking over my shoulder, Betty was trying to catch up to me.

_____

_____

25. To write properly, modifiers can't dangle or be misplaced.

_____

_____

EXERCISE 2

Combine the ideas in each of the following selections into one coherent sentence. Pay special attention to your modifiers.

1. Annette went to her English class.
   Then she went to the library.
   She did not hesitate on her way to the library.

   _____

   _____

2. The class was told to write an 800 word analysis.
   Mike's analysis was 500 words.
   Nancy's analysis was 1000 words.

   _____

   _____

3. Hank got a D+ on his first quiz.
   He got a B− on his second quiz.
   His term mark was C.

   _____

   _____

4. The rowing team made the national finals.
   All the rowers are good athletes.
   They keep in shape year-round.

   _____

   _____

5. I was still awake at 3:00A.M.
   I was working on my essay.
   I was not satisfied with my final draft.

   _____

   _____

BALANCED AND PARALLEL CONSTRUCTIONS

Expository writing often involves balancing information in terms of equations, lists, comparisons, or contrasts. When this material is presented to a reader, it must be composed in such a way that it is clear, consistent, and easy to follow. If the grammatical presentation is balanced, then the reader is free to focus on the relationships within the material being presented.

How is this balance achieved? Grammatically, only a noun can be balanced against a noun; a verb against a verb; a participle against a participle; and so on. This rule is logical and reasonable. Remember the old joke: "What is the difference between an apple and an orange?" "Nothing, except the orange." The same is true of a noun and an adjective; nothing is different except the adjective. Do not equate, list, compare, or contrast different parts of speech. Your argument will be confusing and invalid.

Consider the following types of balanced or parallel constructions:

I. Simple Series

When a list of items is presented in a series, you must use the same grammatical form for each item. In other words, each item should be a noun, or an infinitive, or an adverb, and so on. If this rule is followed, the items are balanced or parallel.

In preparing to write an essay, you must read the primary material, choose a topic, find a thesis, and many other things, if you want to be successful.

What is being listed here? The essay writer must (1) read, (2) choose, (3) find, (4) things. Is this a parallel list? No—the series is verb, verb, verb, *noun.*

In preparing to write an essay, you must <u>read</u> the primary material, <u>choose</u> a topic, <u>find</u> a thesis, and <u>do</u> many other things, if you want to be successful.

Now the writer has listed verb, verb, verb, *verb.* The presentation is balanced and parallel.

The students in the drama class were required to write essays and exams as well as putting on a production.

What are the responsibilities of the students? They are required *to write* and *putting.* Is this parallel? How would you correct it?

The students in the drama class were required <u>to write</u> essays and exams as well as to <u>to put</u> on a production.

OR

The assignments for the drama class included <u>writing</u> essays and exams as well as <u>putting</u> on a production.

Either alternative is preferable to the original, unbalanced sentence. Since the grammar in the corrected sentences is balanced, the content is too.

II. Correlative Conjunctions

Stylistically, the correlative conjunctions (both . . . and; either . . . or; neither . . . nor; not only . . . but also) are effective expository devices. The construction containing correlative conjunctions gives an extra punch to your argument. Your argument is *both* valid *and* strong.

However, you must use this construction in a parallel form, or your argument may be lost. Remember the basic rule of thumb for correlative conjunctions: use the same part of speech or type of construction after each half of the pair. If a noun follows *both*, a noun follows *and*; if an infinitive follows *either*, an infinitive follows *or*; and so on.

Not only should your content be good but also presented clearly.

A clause (should your content be good) follows *not only*; an adjectival past participle and adverb follow *but also*. This is not balanced.

Your content should be <u>not only</u> good, <u>but also</u> presented clearly.

Adjectival constructions follow both *not only* and *but also*.

Othello is both unreasonable and he is extremely jealous.

An adjective follows *both* while a clause follows *and*.

Othello is <u>both</u> unreasonable <u>and</u> extremely jealous.

III. Comparisons

If you compare two or more things, you must use the same parts of speech or the same constructions.

Henry James's sentences are longer than Marshall McLuhan.

This writer has just told you that were you to measure Henry James's sentences you would find that they are more than 72 inches long, since McLuhan is about six feet tall. Compare two possessives here.

<u>Henry James's sentences</u> are longer than <u>Marshall McLuhan's</u>.

As . . . as indicates equality. Both *as's* are necessary.

<u>Paradise Lost</u> is as long if not longer than <u>The Faerie Queene</u>.

Complete the comparison.

<u>Paradise Lost</u> is <u>as</u> long <u>as</u>, if not longer than, <u>The Faerie Queene</u>.

IV. Faulty Ellipsis (Verb Forms)

Sometimes, in order to avoid redundancy, a writer eliminates words. While watching for redundancy is commendable, you cannot eliminate words that are crucial grammatically. Consider the following sentences:

I never have and never shall understand trigonometry.

This sentence sounds all right, but analyse it.

I never have . . .
I never will . . . *understand trigonometry*

"I never have *understand* trigonometry?" It won't work. Understand cannot function as the implied past participle after have.

I never have understood and never shall understand trigonometry.

V. Faulty Ellipsis (Prepositions)

Knowing the meaning of a word and knowing which words should surround it in context are two different things. For example, in English certain verbs and adjectives are followed by particular prepositions. You are surprised *by,* but appalled *at.* Consider complements when you look for synonyms in a dictionary or thesaurus. Be sure you know in what context a word is used.

If you use two or more different verbs or adjectives in a sentence, and these words take different prepositions, you must supply *all* the necessary prepositions.

Freud was both interested and intrigued with the inner workings of the mind.

Yes, Freud was intrigued with, but was he interested *with*? Of course not.

Freud was both interested <u>in</u> and intrigued <u>with</u> the inner workings of the mind.

Idioms are often problematic, especially if they include prepositions. An idiom is an expression which cannot be taken literally. For example, if you *look* something *up,* the direction of your glance is, in fact, *down* as you look in a dictionary. Consider the expressions *look* something *over, look into* something, *look out for* something, and *look after* someone or something. What do the expressions mean? Is *getting away with* a faulty argument the same as *getting away from* it? Be sure you know the idiomatic meanings of expressions before including them in your writing. It is better to *put* a point *across to* your reader than to *put* something *over on* him or her.

VI. Antithetical Sentences and Arguments

Well balanced, antithetical statements provide wit, point, and conciseness in your writing. The balance on a pivotal point makes for neat, clear reading and easy assimilation of the material.

Do not despair: one of the thieves was saved; do not exult: one of the thieves was damned.

The balanced antithesis balances on a semicolon.

Consider Oscar Wilde's assessment of remarriage:

When a woman marries again, it is because she detested her first husband; when a man marries again, it is because he adored his first wife. Women try their luck; men risk theirs.

Perhaps Wilde's sentiment is questionable, but his presentation is certainly clear.

Balanced antithetical sentences are particularly valuable in comparative situations:

In <u>Paradise Lost</u> the hero is either Satan or Adam; in <u>Paradise Regained</u> the hero is clearly Christ.

RECAP

Balance your presentation; include what is crucial for balance and omit what is not. Equate, list, compare, or contrast the same parts of speech. Then *not only* will you write, *but also* you will write well.

EXERCISE 1

The material in the following sentences is not balanced or parallel. Find the problems and then correct them.

1. The writer can therefore be described as self-centred and an introvert.

_____

_____

2. The first conflict is between the state and the individual; the second is a moral conflict within the man himself; the third is the conflict of man versus man.

_____

_____

3. The character is unselfish. He would rather please another than to avoid an unpleasantry in his own life.

_____

_____

4. The assignments for the literature course are heavier than the physics course.

_____

_____

5. You can either read one novel or the other.

_____

_____

6. I was distressed and concerned about the errors and typing.

_____

_____

7. Susan's marks are as good if not better than her sister.

_____

_____

8. The book is about travelling and strange cultures.

_____

_____

9. One must be loyal to himself, to his family, and his country.

_____

_____

10. I was offended when the instructor told me I either hadn't studied or I was not intelligent.

_____

_____

11. It is difficult to decide between going to the party or to see the new film at the Odeon.

_____

_____

12. I looked for that word in both the dictionary and in the thesaurus.

_____

_____

13. Finding a book in the library required perseverance and understanding the floor plan.

_____

_____

14. The final step is proofreading the essay and to hand it in.

_____

_____

15. My car uses more gas than Jim.

_____

_____

16. Samantha is not only very intelligent but also she studies very hard.

_____

_____

17. Milton both wrote poetry and prose.

_____

_____

18. My thesis required more research than Thomas, yet I finished before he did.

_____

_____

19. I always have and always shall be careful of my punctuation.

_____

_____

20. The instructor let Ted's seminar go longer than I did.

_____

_____

21. I have neither sympathy nor will I make excuses for students who fail because they plagiarize.

_____

_____

22. The characters in his later novels are not as developed as his early ones.

_____

_____

23. It bothers me that Heather never has and never will take her courses seriously.

_____

_____

24. I looked for that book both in the university and the city library.

_____

_____

25. The reader is, at the same time, both distressed and interested in Satan's actions at this point in the epic.

_____

_____

EXERCISE 2

Combine the ideas in each of the following selections into one coherent sentence. Be especially careful that your presentation is balanced.

1. George is a friend of mine.
   He is Helen's friend too.
   He is an accomplished pianist.
   He also golfs well.

   _____

   _____

2. I accomplished a great deal today.
   I cleaned my apartment.
   Another thing I did was proofread my essay.

   _____

   _____

3. Gloria's family is pleased about her approaching marriage to Alex.
   The marriage pleases Alex's family too.

   _____

   _____

4. We were surprised by the film's ending.
   The film was very suspenseful.
   We were frightened.
   We were also astonished.

   _____

   _____

5. The cafeteria where we usually eat was closed.
   The other cafeterias were closed too.
   We went to a restaurant downtown.

   _____

   _____

CHAPTER 10

Punctuation and Related Sentence Structure Problems

Man spoke before he wrote. We all speak much more than we write; but, whether we speak or write, we indicate when one thought stops and another begins. Orally, this is done through voice modulation. In writing, this is done through punctuation. Thus, in many instances when oral speech would require a pause or a stop, written speech employs a punctuation mark, generally a comma or a period. Breath pauses are not the only excuses for punctuation; *logical rules* govern the use of punctuation marks. Generally, however, if a logical unit of expression is completed, punctuation indicates this completion.

Terminal punctuation is no real problem. You know you end a sentence with a period, a question mark, or an exclamation mark. Then you are free to begin a new thought in the next sentence. Internal punctuation poses more of a problem; you must decide both where to place the punctuation, and which mark to use. This chapter deals with the three most common kinds of internal punctuation: the comma, the semicolon, and the colon. In addition, the apostrophe, the dash, the parenthesis, and the hyphen are considered.

It is imperative that you punctuate correctly. Punctuation cannot be avoided. If you persistently misuse the comma, for example, your analysis or essay will probably have fifty to one hundred errors. Although these are the same error repeated, you give the impression of making more than a single error and you irritate the reader.

Since punctuation does, in fact, permeate writing, it is worthwhile to consider the rules of punctuation. It really is not so intimidating a prospect as it appears at first glance. Punctuation is logical; assimilate the logic and you should be comfortable with your punctuation in your writing.

THE COMMA (,)

The comma consistently presents problems to writers. It is either omitted when it should be used, or used when it should be omitted. Comma usage is not a difficult concept to grasp. When there is *legitimate cause* to pause, use a comma. Rationalize the *legitimacy* of your pausing by noting the completion of a logical unit. Too many pauses result in uneven writing. If there is *good reason* to pause, pause; if there is not, do not.

Consider the following rules;

I. Conjunctions join. In English, there are six conjunctions: *and, but, for, or, nor, yet*. As conjunctions, these words join equal grammatical elements—nouns and nouns, verbs and verbs, clauses and clauses, and the like. If you memorize this list of conjunctions, you will make life as a writer much easier for yourself.

When a conjunction joins independent clauses (sentences which can stand on their own and contain at least a subject and a verb), a comma is used *before the conjunction.*

The course was difficult but interesting.

But joins two adjectives, *not* two independent clauses. No comma is necessary.

The course was difficult, but it was interesting as well.

Here *but* joins two independent clauses. A comma precedes *but*.

We ate dinner and dessert.

Here *and* joins two nouns.

We ate dinner, and then we ate dessert.

And joins two independent clauses and is preceded by a comma.

II. In a list or series of items, commas separate all terms in the list, including the last two. Often separating the last two items is optional. However, in 95% of the cases a comma is preferable; in the other 5% it is not incorrect. Use the comma between all terms in the series.

The child started the car, put it in gear, and drove into the wall.

Commas separate verb phrases in this sentence.

He likes caviar, escargots, and wieners.

Here each noun in the series is separated by a comma.

III. Often, especially in expository prose, a sentence opens or closes with material which is useful, explanatory, or relevant, but not *crucial* in terms of either form or content. Such material may be labelled *parenthetical.* When it appears at the beginning of a sentence it is set off with a comma. It is necessary to set off the opener from the crucial clause of the sentence. Thus, subordinate material is subordinated.

When class started, the fire alarm went off.

In spite of the heat, she insisted on wearing her new fur coat.

In each of the preceding sentences, the parenthetical material is set off with a comma.

IV. Parenthetical materials at the end of sentences require analysis before you decide on their punctuation (or absence of punctuation). Subordinate material at the conclusion of a sentence is not treated as a parenthetical afterthought.

The fire alarm went off when class started.

She insisted on wearing her new fur coat in spite of the heat.

An *afterthought,* however as a concluding comment in a sentence *is* set off. If the afterthought is included for emphasis, or if it is not subordinate to the rest of the sentence, it is set off with a comma. Consider the following sentence.

He became disinterested in her obviously.

If *obviously* is not separated as an afterthought in this sentence, *obviously* appears to be part of the female anatomy.

He became disinterested in her, obviously.

Here, *obviously* is an adverbial afterthought.

Afterthoughts are sometimes emphatic. In this case they require punctuation to set them off.

The lecture was on the Elizabethans, especially Marlowe.

She loves her liquor, gin in particular.

The afterthoughts must be separated from the main sentence.

V. Like parenthetical openers and closers, parenthetical insertions must be set off from the rest of the sentence. While only one comma is necessary for the openers and closers, insertions require a *pair of commas* to set off the parenthetical material.

The queen, Elizabeth II, is the head of state for all the Commonwealth countries.

Elizabeth II is in apposition. We know who the queen is; therefore, her name is parenthetical material and is set off with a pair of commas.

Tennyson, who wrote <u>In Memoriam</u>, is a Victorian poet.

Who wrote in Memoriam is a relative clause referring to Tennyson. The clause is not crucial; it gives information about Tennyson, but the information is parenthetical. A *pair* of commas is necessary.

NOTE: Only parenthetical material is set off by commas. Crucial material requires no punctuation.

Book IX, which relates the fall of Adam and Eve, is very dramatic.

BUT

The book which relates the fall of Adam and Eve is very dramatic.

Book IX is *particular*. A reader of *Paradise Lost* could determine that the writer of the sentence is referring to the fall of Adam and Eve. The clause *which relates the fall of Adam and Eve* is further particularizing a particular. The information is parenthetical.

The book is general. The writer of the sentence could mean any one of twelve books. The clause *which relates the fall of Adam and Eve* particularizes a general, defines the book as Book IX. No internal punctuation is necessary.

Consider the following pairs of sentences:

Anderson, the N.D.P. candidate, won the election.

The man who ran for the N.D.P. won the election.

My only sister, Susan, is here for the weekend.

My sister Susan is here for the weekend. (I have three sisters.)

You now know both when *to* and when *not to* use a comma. If you cannot rationalize the use of the comma by one of the four comma rules, don't use one. One place in particular where a comma is *not* necessary is between a subject and verb when there is no parenthetical material between the two.

Agatha Christie, wrote many books.

This is a common error. Avoid it at all costs.

THE SEMICOLON (;)

The semicolon is stronger than the comma. While the comma pauses, the semicolon stops. Notice the formation of the semicolon; it is a comma with a period over it. This piece of punctuation is used in three instances.

I. A semicolon is used to separate independent statements or clauses. Rather than joining them with a comma and a conjunction, the writer may use a semicolon *if* the two statements are related in thought. This is a much more sophisticated presentation than ending the first statement with a period, then beginning a new sentence. The semicolon tells the reader that the sentences are related in thought.

In Paradise Lost the hero is either Satan or Adam; in Paradise Regained the hero is clearly Christ.

You might use a period to separate the two independent clauses. On the other hand, since they are closely related in thought, a *semicolon* is preferable. A *comma* is not sufficient here; the comma would need the added strength of a conjunction.

In Paradise Lost the hero is either Satan or Adam, but in Paradise Regained the hero is clearly Christ.

II. *Conjunctive adverbs* are linking words. Every good expository writer should use them to guide his or her reader's chain of thought. Linking words are signposts indicating the direction an argument is taking. A good writer has a repertoire of verbal signposts.

When two independent clauses are joined by a conjunctive adverb, a semicolon precedes the adverb and a comma follows it.

The principal conjunctive adverbs are the following: therefore, however, also, in addition, furthermore, consequently, subsequently, besides, anyhow, as a result, indeed, in fact, instead, for example, hence, meanwhile, otherwise, moreover, then, thus.

This list is not exhaustive. There are many more words or phrases that may be used as conjunctive adverbs. Think of some. Can you list ten? Try. List them here and consider how you would use them in sentences.

1. _____   6. _____

2. _____   7. _____

3. _____   8. _____

4. _____   9. _____

5. _____   10. _____

Remember the six conjunctions (and, but, for, or, nor, yet). If a joining word is not one of these six, it is listed as a conjunctive adverb and requires a semicolon. In complex sentences, the pivotal comma may be promoted to semicolon and the conjunction may serve the function of a conjunctive adverb.

On first reading, Blake's Songs of Innocence *may seem simplistic; however, closer examination will prove this work to be very complex.*

However is a conjunctive adverb joining two sentences. Note the punctuation.

NOTE: Linking words do not always link clauses. They are not always used *conjunctively*; sometimes they are merely adverbial parenthetical expressions.

The solution, therefore, is simple.

Therefore is an adverb serving as a parenthetical insertion.

III. A comma is used to separate all items in a series, including the last two. If, however, the *items* in the series are especially long, or if they themselves are internally punctuated, semicolons are used to separate the items.

The seasons are spring, summer, fall, and winter.

The four items in this series are separated by commas.

The seasons are spring, when trees bud; summer, when everything is in blossom; fall, when the leaves change colour and fall from the trees; and winter, when the trees are bare.

Each of the four items is long and internally punctuated; therefore, semicolons separate the items.

NOTE: The issue is long *items,* not long *lists.*

There are, then, three basic rules for use of the semicolon: on its own, separating *related* independent clauses; with a conjunctive adverb, separating independent clauses; and separating long items in a list. Except in Rule III, which is a special case in complex sentences, the semicolon is used instead of a period. It stops. The semicolon is a very useful piece of punctuation. Use it well and your writing will improve.

THE COLON (:)

The colon is a capital semicolon on your typewriter. Like the semicolon, it has three uses. However, these uses are distinct from those of the semicolon. The colon points forward to further elucidation of a point or argument while the semicolon stops. In learning its three uses, you will become aware of both *where* and *where not* to use a colon.

I. If a list is introduced by a complete sentence, a colon precedes the list. This is the case *only if* the introductory material could stand on its own as a complete sentence. Compare the following sentences:

I am enjoying the course because we are working with Eliot and Yeats, my favourite writers.

BUT

I am enjoying the course because we are working with my two favourite writers: Eliot and Yeats.

The seasons are spring, summer, fall, and winter.

BUT

There are four seasons: spring, summer, fall, and winter.

In the first of each pair of sentences, the list is not introduced by a complete sentence. No colon precedes the list. However, in the second of each pair of sentences, the list is introduced by a complete sentence; thus, a colon is used.

II. When two independent clauses are written and the second is more than just related in thought to the first, a colon separates the two. If the second clause explains or gives the reasons for the first, the colon is the pivotal piece of punctuation. Remember—while the semicolon halts, the colon moves forward.

Harry was despondent: the roof was leaking, the cat was having kittens, and his wife had left home.

Notice that the second clause answers the hypothetical question "Why?" which might be asked after the first. The colon says, "Why? I'll tell you."

I need help: my essay is due tomorrow and I haven't found a topic yet.

III. If a quotation is introduced by a complete sentence, a colon introduces the quotation. Only if a *complete sentence* introduces the quotation is a colon used. Consider the following example:

The witches set the stage for the moral paradox in Macbeth: "Fair is foul, and foul is fair. Hover through the fog and filthy air" (Macbeth I.i.11–12).

A complete sentence introduces the quotation, and a colon is used.

You are now familiar with the three basic uses of the colon: before a list; between complete sentences when the second gives the reasons for the first; and before quotations which are introduced by a complete sentence.

The comma, the semicolon, and the colon are the principal pieces of punctuation used in formal writing. They have, among them, only eleven rules which indicate both when *to* punctuate and when *not to* punctuate. Familiarity with these rules should become so habitual that you should not have to think about them.

The less common pieces of punctuation (the dash, the parenthesis, and the hyphen), along with the apostrophe, will be reviewed here. Use these marks cautiously and sparingly, but do not be afraid to use them.

THE APOSTROPHE

I. The apostrophe shows possession. The aprostrophe followed by *s* indicates possession:

Chaucer's England
Keats's poetry
Dickens' novels

NOTE: When a name or a singular noun ends in *s*, you must decide whether to use *'s* or just an apostrophe. Consider the natural sound, and decide whether the *'s* would be sounded or not. You would say "Keats's poetry," but would not add an additional styllable to "Dickens' novels."

To indicate plural possession, the plural of the noun is written. If the noun ends in *s*, an apostrophe is added:

writers' union
students' essays

If, however, the plural of the noun does not end in *s*, then apostrophe *s* is added.

men's room
mice's cheese

II. The apostrophe followed by *s* is used to pluralize a number, a letter, a sign, or an abbreviation.

He wrote in the 1890's.
I hope to get all A's and B's.

III. The apostrophe is used in contractions. *HOWEVER*, contractions are generally avoided in formal writing assignments. In *informal* writing, an apostrophe indicates the omission of a letter or letters.

I   can't do this work.
   cannot

Why   aren't the essays finished?
     are not

DO NOT use the apostrophe merely to pluralize nouns. *S* alone does that.

EXCEPTIONS TO THE RULE

Its and *whose* are possessive pronouns *without* apostrophes. *It's* means *it is*; *who's* means *who is*. They are contractions.

There is a place for everything, and everything should be in its place.

The man whose rib was donated is Adam.

THE DASH (—)

The dash is a long line when you write, and *two hyphens* when you type. Like a comma, it sets off material. However, while a comma says "Pause," a dash says "Take a breath." If you use too many dashes your essay will be breathless and your sentences will appear fragmented, but an occasional dash adds variety.

I. The dash emphasizes a sudden break in thought in a sentence.

Joyce's characteristic narrative mode—the mode which he perfected—is stream of consciousness.

The dashes here are more emphatic than commas.

II. The dash sets off and emphasizes a summarizing or particularizing word or phrase at the end of a sentence.

There is only one word to describe Shakespeare's gift—genius.

This emphasis at the end of the sentence is effective if this construction is used *sparingly.*

PARENTHESES

I. Parentheses are less emphatic than dashes in setting off *very* parenthetical material. The parentheses may be used *instead of commas.*

Donne (the most famous of the Metaphysical Poets) has a distinctive style.

Note the absence of commas.

II. Cross references or informal page references are enclosed in parentheses.

His development may be illustrated on a graph (see Appendix B).

The reader is referred to another section or page of the essay.

THE HYPHEN (-)

I. The hyphen is used to form compound modifiers of nouns or pronouns when they immediately precede the word they are modifying.

She is a hard-working student with a never-say-die attitude.

II. The hyphen separates a word syllabically when it must be separated at the end of a line or script or type.

He developed an individual style because he would not con-
form to traditional modes of expression.

Be sure to divide a word into syllables before hyphenating it.

NOTE: A syllable generally starts with a consonant, *rather than* with a vowel unless it is the first syllable in a word. Bear this in mind when you decide where to hyphenate.

While punctuation plays a major role in writing, its rules are logical and consistent. Punctuation guides the reader and makes written material manageable since it is divided into major and minor ideas. Badly punctuated material is almost impossible to read. Thus, if you do not punctuate well, you will waste your ideas.

EXERCISE 1

Consider the punctuation in the following sentences. In some instances you must omit punctuation; in others you must add it; in yet others, no corrections are necessary.

1. He had always associated singing with happy times, but found that this was not so; singing could express grief and sadness as well.
2. In "Clay" by James Joyce music is a ritual used to cover up moments of tension and distress.
3. People, who live in glass houses, shouldn't throw stones.
4. Many go to college from sheer inertia. Not being able to think of anything else to do,
5. The winter he pointed out would bring increased suffering to the unemployed.
6. Robinson Crusoe, was on a ship which was wrecked; he was the sole survivor.
7. I work for two reasons, to make money and to keep busy.
8. This opinion might be well substantiated however I still feel the end of the novel destroy's the slow building of Hucks social conscience, it makes a mockery of it.
9. Dignity and caution told him to stop, he was not listening.
10. Jubilee being the nearest small town; it lies a few miles south.
11. A musician, is able to bring joy to persons, close to him. But a writer has a more difficult task, his audience, is sitting, far away from him. He can't play soft music to express his emotions: he must write, something which readers can identify.
12. Language is the focal point of Elizabethan drama: the emphasis is placed on words rather than narrative; expression is more important than content.
13. These people are all unable to do anything about the tragedies occurring to those they love but they are all sincere in their feelings and anguished over their impotence.
14. Like Richard II and Falstaff, Richard III is a convincingly fine actor who can change his face to suit the occasion. The wooing of Lady Anne a scene which verges upon burlesque is a primary example of Richard's dazzling, hypnotic technique.
15. Through a rendering, of the underlying emotions, which contribute to the elements of both war and peace; Homer, has painted, a graphic picture of the factors which constitute: a warring or a peaceful society.

FREQUENT SENTENCE STRUCTURE AND PUNCTUATION PROBLEMS

As you have seen in doing the preceding exercise, sentences which are incorrectly punctuated are difficult to read. Either they are overpunctuated and jumpy or staccato, or they are underpunctuated and long-winded. Possible errors in punctuation are limitless. There are, however, three frequent sentence structure-punctuation errors: the run-on sentence, the comma splice, and the sentence fragment. These particular errors have probably used up more red ink from markers' pens than all other errors combined. Avoid these problem areas by applying punctuation rules.

The Run-on Sentence

When you get deeply involved in the material you are committing to paper, your ideas come quite quickly. If you merge two complete sentences without indicating where one thought stops and the next starts, you have *run-on* your sentences. You leave your reader in a quandary. He or she does not know where to stop and start again.

> *This poem is by Alexander Pope it is written in heroic couplets.*
>
> These two sentences are merged to make one run-on sentence. The error can be corrected in a variety of ways.

1. Write two complete sentences.

   This poem is by Alexander Pope. It is written in heroic couplets.

2. Use a conjunction and a comma to separate the two ideas.

   This poem is by Alexander Pope, and it is written in heroic couplets.

3. If the two ideas are related in thought, separate them with a semicolon.

   This poem is by Alexander Pope; it is written in heroic couplets.

4. Subordinate one major idea and make it a parenthetical or a non-parenthetical expression.

   This poem, which is written in heroic couplets, is by Alexander Pope.

   This poem by Alexander Pope is written in heroic couplets.

The methods of correcting the run-on sentence are progressively more sophisticated. Be comfortable with each solution, and use the most suitable method as you correct your errors.

The Comma Splice

While run-on sentences provide no interruption between complete thoughts, the comma splice provides insufficient interruption. Sentences that are fused or *spliced* with a comma cannot stand either together or separately. Avoid comma splices.

Like the run-on sentence, the comma splice can be corrected in a variety of ways.

In the first act Macbeth is honourable, in the second he is dishonourable.

Consider these corrections:

1. Write two complete sentences.

   In the first act Macbeth is honourable. In the second he is dishonourable.

2. Use a conjunction along with the comma to separate the two ideas.

   In the first act Macbeth is honourable, but in the second he is dishonourable.

3. If the two ideas are related in thought, separate them with a semicolon.

   In the first act Macbeth is honourable; in the second he is dishonourable.

4. Subordinate one major idea and make it a parenthetical or non-parenthetical expression.

   Although he is honourable in the first act, Macbeth is dishonourable in the second.

   Macbeth, who is honourable in the first act, is dishonourable in the second.

Remember that a comma is relatively weak. It does not have the strength on its own to separate independent clauses. Use either a conjunction (with a comma) or a semicolon.

The Sentence Fragment

The run-on sentence and the comma splice are one end of the spectrum of sentence structure errors. In them, the writer gives too much information for a single sentence; there are too many principal nouns and verbs. A sentence fragment is the other end of the spectrum. Either a subject or a principal verb is missing. Verbals are not verbs; therefore a participle or gerund cannot be a predicate.

There are two ways of correcting a sentence fragment: you can either supply what is missing to make an independent clause or subordinate the fragment, attaching it to the preceding or following sentence.

Swift wrote both poetry and prose. Being more famous for his prose.

Being is not a verb; it is a verbal. In addition, there is no subject for the fragment.

Swift wrote both poetry and prose. He is more famous for his prose.

Swift wrote both poetry and prose, his prose being better known.

Be sure that every sentence you write has at least a subject and a predicate. A verbal cannot be a predicate.

EXERCISE 1

The following sentences have either run-on, comma splice, or sentence fragment errors. Find the problems and correct them. Attempt various ways of making corrections, finding the best expression for each idea.

1. Shakespeare's comic spirit encourages us to feel delight in and reverence for life. Laughter or interior smiles being concomitant to this spirit.
   are.

   _____

   _____

   _____

2. Cleopatra is the consummate seductress, in spite of her opulence, playfulness, and languidness in love, she never lacks dignity.

   _____

   _____

   _____

3. Religion playing a minor role in Del's life; she has no real concern for it.

   _____

   _____

4. The intent of the last chapter being to ridicule the romantic tradition, and to win sympathy for the realistic hero Huck Finn.

   _____

   _____

   _____

5. Mrs. Mooney appears to be a very strick and moral person. Someone who wants her child to be in only the best surroundings.

   _____

   _____

   _____

6. Whereas some six million tons of shipping were destroyed. Eight million tons under construction more than offset the loss.

   _____

   _____

   _____

7. I am taking three science courses: biology, chemistry, and physics. In addition English and history.

   _____

   _____

8. This poem is a sonnet it has fourteen lines.

   _____

9. I plan to teach. Or maybe go into publishing.

   _____

10. I read the advertisement on a matchbook. Success without college, I sent for the brochure.

    _____

    _____

11. Christ serves the functions of a scapegoat, Willie Loman does too.

    _____

    _____

12. I manage to keep busy. Reading, watching television, or visiting friends.

    _____

    _____

13. The course work is heavy. Four essays and two exams.

    _____

14. In addition, a philosophical question which has never been answered satisfactorily.

    _____

    _____

15. It could be said that he is working on the assumption that virtue not challenged is not virtue at all, the strong will be victorious while the weak will fall prey to evil.

_____

_____

_____

16. In some of Donne's earlier love poems, death as an image of sleep, effective until the lovers are reawakened and reunited in the after life.

_____

_____

_____

17. He looked at many types of cars. Sports models to station wagons.

_____

_____

18. He is very intelligent and he works diligently. Which is why he is successful.

_____

_____

19. I love to cook. Especially for company.

_____

20. Some people learn languages easily, some have to struggle to learn.

_____

_____

21. I enjoy the works on the reading list. The short stories in particular.

_____

_____

22. To err is human. To forgive divine.

_____

23. I told him to be careful he wouldn't listen.

_____

24. Duddy, appears in two of Richler's novel's; *The Apprenticeship of Duddy Kravitz* and *St. Urbain's Horesman.*

_____

_____

_____

25. Its not whether you win or lose, its how you play the game.

_____

_____

Metre

WHAT IS IT?

Rhythm is always expressive. Metre establishes rhythm. All language, spoken, written, or thought, has a metrical pattern. This pattern is composed of stressed and unstressed syllables. The stresses are determined by the word root and by usage. A dictionary gives this information. In English, most words have only one metrical pattern.

Scansion is the analysis of metre and depends on both meaning and sentence structure. Consider the rhythm of the following piece:

> 'Twas brillig, and the slithy toves
> Did gyre and gimble in the wabe.
> (*Alice in Wonderland*)

Here it is your sense of sentence structure which makes you able to identify parts of speech and to "know" how to pronounce the words and so scan the lines.

PROSE AND POETRY

Prose rhythm is highly irregular; in fact, regularity is thought to detract from the effect of prose and is used only for special effects, such as rhetoric and humour.

In *poetic prose,* the rhythm is more regular than in prose. That is, there are clearly identifiable units which are repeated. Consider, for example, the 23rd Psalm in which there are many parallel constructions which have similar, if not identical, metrical patterns:

The Lord is my shepherd; I shall not want.
He maketh me to lie down in green pastures:
he leadeth me beside the still waters.
He restoreth my soul:
he leadeth me in the paths of righteousness for his name's sake.

Yea, though I walk through the valley of the shadow of death,
I will fear no evil:
for thou art with me;
thy rod and thy staff they comfort me.

Though preparest a table for me in the presence of mine enemies:
thou anointest my head with oil;
my cup runneth over.

Surely goodness and mercy shall follow me all the days of my life:
and I will dwell in the house of the Lord for ever.

In *free verse,* rhythmic regularity is even more prevalent than in poetic prose. The metrical unit is not the line, as in poetry, but the stanza or "verse envelope." The rhythm which results from this large unit is called cadence. The distinction between poetic prose and free verse is often difficult and depends on the way it looks on the page as well as on the reader's experience with other examples of these two forms.

> Presentiment—is that long shaden—on the Lawn—
> Indicative that Suns go down—
>
> The Notice to the startled Grass
> That Darkness—is about to pass—
>
> (Dickinson)

In *metrical verse,* the metre is determined by scanning a line or a number of lines to discover the basic pattern (the type and number of feet per line). There are more than 30 kinds of metrical units or feet in English, but six are common:

-/	iamb(ic)
/-	trochee (trochaic)
--/	anapest(ic)
/--	dactyl(ic)
--	pyrrhic
//	spondee (spondaic)

The number of feet per line contributes to the basic pattern:

1 foot - monometer (unusual)
2 feet - dimeter
3 feet - trimeter
4 feet - tetrameter
5 feet - pentameter
6 feet - hexameter
7 feet - heptameter
8 feet - octameter

(The pyrrhic and spondaic are not commonly used to form a line of verse.)

In common practice, the number of *stressed* syllables determines the length of a line. The foot is a metrical unit in poetry and has *no existence* outside the line.

In every poem, the basic metre is the pattern a poet *chooses.* It is the one you can count out as you count the beats in music. Integrated with this basic metre is a rhythmic pattern derived from the meaning of the words. This rhythm of meaning furnishes a counterpoint to the base metre, as in jazz. The basic metre is always there, but the poet works with words to develop variations which serve specific purposes, or should. One way of spotting a bad poem is to demonstrate that the basic metre is inappropriate or that the rhythmic variations are not functional. *These "irregularities," in a good poem, are produced by design and not by accident.* The reader participates by discovering the significant prosody of the poem. The critic's job is to show what purpose is served by (1) the choice of a basic pattern, and (2) irregularities or variations on that basic pattern.

THE PURPOSE OF METRE

Hopkins described poetry as "speech formed . . . to be heard for its own sake and interest even over and above its interest of meaning." Metre is pleasurable in the same way melody in music or composition in painting are. They are all stimulating to one or more senses; metre in poetry appeals to both the eye and the ear. The pleasure has something to do with expectation—our idea of the way it "should" sound.

Furthermore, metre is one of the signs by which we recognize poetry and music as art forms. Metre "distances" the created world of the imagination so that we can recognize in these art forms abstractions and condensations of experience in the everyday world without confusing the two kinds of life. Since metre is an "abstracting" device, it is one method of controlling powerful emotion (upon which poetry depends) so that we can perceive the *significance* of the emotional idea and not simply by shocked or overwhelmed by it.

Index